W. L. (William Livingston) Alden

The Cruise of the Canoe Club

W. L. (William Livingston) Alden

The Cruise of the Canoe Club

ISBN/EAN: 9783743308053

Manufactured in Europe, USA, Canada, Australia, Japa

Cover: Foto ©ninafisch / pixelio.de

Manufactured and distributed by brebook publishing software (www.brebook.com)

W. L. (William Livingston) Alden

The Cruise of the Canoe Club

"DON'T THINK FOR A MOMENT OF GETTING ANY OTHER CANOE." [P. 12.

The Cruise of the Canoe Club

By W. L. ALDEN
AUTHOR OF
"A NEW ROBINSON CRUSOE"

ILLUSTRATED

NEW YORK AND LONDON
HARPER & BROTHERS PUBLISHERS

HARPER'S YOUNG PEOPLE SERIES

SIXTY-CENT EDITION

FRANCONIA STORIES
By Jacob Abbott
- Malleville
- Mary Bell
- Ellen Linn
- Wallace
- Beechnut
- Stuyvesant
- Agnes
- Mary Erskine
- Rodolphus
- Caroline

By W. L. Alden
- The Moral Pirates
- The Cruise of the "Ghost"
- The Cruise of the Canoe Club
- The Adventures of Jimmy Brown
- Jimmy Brown Trying to Find Europe
- A New Robinson Crusoe

By James Barnes
- The Blockaders

By William Black
- The Four Macnicols

By Lewis Carroll
- Alice's Adventures in Wonderland
- Through the Looking-Glass
- The Hunting of the Snark

By Col. W. F. Cody
- The Adventures of Buffalo Bill

By George C. Eggleston
- Strange Stories from History

By John Habberton
- Who Was Paul Grayson?

By Mrs. W. J. Hays
- Prince Lazybones
- The Princess Idleways

By George A. Henty
- In the Hands of the Cave-Dwellers

By Ernest Ingersoll
- The Ice Queen

By David Ker
- The Lost City
- Into Unknown Seas

By Lucy C. Lillie
- Mildred's Bargain
- Nan
- Jo's Opportunity

- Phil and the Baby
- False Witness
- Rolf House
- Music and Musicians
- The Colonel's Money
- The Household of Glen Holly

By Livingston B. Morse
- The Road to Nowhere

By Miss Mulock
- The Little Lame Prince
- The Adventures of a Brownie
- Little Sunshine's Holiday
- The Cousin from India
- Twenty Years Ago
- Is It True?
- Miss Moore
- An Only Sister

By Kirk Munroe
- Wakulla
- The Flamingo Feather
- Derrick Sterling
- Chrystal, Jack & Co.

By James Otis
- Mr. Stubbs's Brother
- Tim and Tip
- Toby Tyler; or, Ten Weeks with a Circus
- Raising the "Pearl"
- Silent Pete; or, the Stowaways
- Left Behind; or, Ten Days a Newsboy

By G. B. Perry
- Uncle Peter's Trust

By L. C. Pyrnelle
- Diddie, Dumps, and Tot

By Margaret E. Sangster
- Little Knights and Ladies—Poems

By W. O. Stoddard
- Two Arrows
- The Red Mustang
- The Talking Leaves

By Sophie Swett
- Captain Polly

Illustrated. Price, per volume, 60 cents

HARPER & BROTHERS, PUBLISHERS, NEW YORK

Copyright, 1883, by Harper & Brothers.

All rights reserved

ILLUSTRATIONS.

	PAGE
"Don't Think for a Moment of Getting any other Canoe"	*Frontispiece*
"She's Half Full of Water"	30
A Stampede in Camp	38
Not so Easy as it Looks	50
"He Caught Hold of the Root of a Tree and kept his Canoe Stationary"	70
Running the Rapid	78
Getting Breakfast under Difficulties	94
Hunting for a Wild-cat in Chambly Castle	110
Sailing Down the Richelieu River	116
"They Found a Bear Feasting upon the Remains of their Breakfast"	138
Around the Camp-fire	146
"How in the World did you Get up there?"	160

THE CRUISE

OF

THE CANOE CLUB.

Chapter I.

IT is a very easy thing for four boys to make up their minds to get four canoes and to go on a canoe cruise, but it is not always so easy to carry out such a project—as Charley Smith, Tom Schuyler, Harry Wilson, and Joe Sharpe discovered.

Canoes cost money; and though some canoes cost more than others, it is impossible to buy a new wooden canoe of an approved model for less than seventy-five dollars. Four canoes, at seventy-five dollars each, would cost altogether three hundred dollars. As the entire amount of pocket-money in the possession of the boys was only seven dollars and thirteen cents, it was clear that they were not precisely in a position to buy canoes.

There was Harry's uncle, who had already furnished his nephew and his young comrades first with a row-boat, and then with a sail-boat. Even a benevolent uncle deserves some mercy, and the boys agreed that it would never do to ask Uncle John to spend three hundred dollars in canoes for them. "The most we can ask of him," said Charley Smith, "is to let us sell the *Ghost* and use the money to help pay for canoes."

Now, the *Ghost*, in which the boys had made a cruise along the south shore of Long Island, was a very nice sail-boat, but it was improbable that any one would be found who would be willing to give more than two hundred dollars for her. There would still be a hundred dollars wanting, and the prospect of finding that sum seemed very small.

"If we could only have stayed on that water-logged brig and brought her into port we should have made lots of money," said Tom. "The captain of the schooner that towed us home went back with a steamer and brought the brig in yesterday. Suppose we go and look at her once more?"

While cruising in the *Ghost* the boys had found an abandoned brig, which they had tried to sail into New York harbor, but they had been compelled to give up the task, and to hand her over to the captain of a schooner which towed the partly disabled *Ghost* into port. They all thought they would like to see the brig again, so they went down to Burling Slip, where she was lying, and went on board her.

The captain of the schooner met the boys on the dock. He was in excellent spirits, for the brig was loaded with valuable South American timber, and he was sure of receiving as much as ten thousand dollars from her owners. He knew very well that, while the boys had no legal right to any of the money, they had worked hard in trying to save the brig, and had been the means of putting her in his way. He happened to be an honest, generous man, and he felt very rich; so he insisted on making each of the boys a present.

The present was sealed up in an envelope, which he gave to Charley Smith, telling him not to look at its contents until after dinner—the boys having mentioned that they were all to take dinner together at Uncle John's house. Charley put the envelope rather carelessly in his pocket; but when it was opened it was found to contain four new one-hundred-dollar bills.

It need hardly be said that the boys were delighted. They showed the money to Uncle John, who told them that they had fairly earned it, and need feel no hesitation about accepting it. They had now money enough to buy canoes, and to pay the expenses of a canoe cruise. Mr. Schuyler, Mr. Sharpe, and Charley's guardian were consulted, and at Uncle John's request gave their consent to the canoeing scheme. The first great difficulty in the way was thus entirely removed.

"I don't know much about canoes," remarked Uncle John, when the boys asked his advice as to what kind of canoes they should get, "but I know the commodore of a canoe club. You had better go and see him, and follow his advice. I'll give you a letter of introduction to him."

No time was lost in finding the commodore, and Charley Smith explained to him that four young canoeists would like to know what was the very best kind of canoe for them to get.

The Commodore, who, in spite of his magnificent title, wasn't in the least alarming, laughed, and said, "That is a question that I've made up my mind never to try to answer. But I'll give you the names of four canoeists, each of whom uses a different variety of canoe. You go and see them, listen to what they say, believe it all, and then come back and see me, and we'll come to a decision." He then wrote four notes of introduction, gave them to the boys, and sent them away.

The first canoeist to whom the boys were referred

received them with great kindness, and told them that it was fortunate they had come to him. "The canoe that you want," said he, "is the 'Rice Lake' canoe, and if you had gone to somebody else, and he had persuaded you to buy 'Rob Roy' canoes or 'Shadows,' you would have made a great mistake. The 'Rice Lake' canoe is nearly flat-bottomed, and so stiff that there is no danger that you will capsize her. She paddles easily, and sails faster than any other canoe. She is roomy, and you can carry about twice as much in her as you can carry in a 'Rob Roy.' She has no keel, so that you can run rapids easily in her, and she is built in a peculiar way that makes it impossible for her to leak. Don't think for a moment of getting any other canoe, for if you do you will never cease to regret it."

He was such a pleasant, frank gentleman, and was so evidently earnest in what he said, that the boys at once decided to get 'Rice Lake' canoes. They did not think it worth while to make any farther inquiries; but, as they had three other notes of introduction with them, Tom Schuyler said that it would hardly do to throw them away. So they went to see the next canoeist, though without the least expectation that he would say anything that would alter their decision.

Canoeist No. 2 was as polite and enthusiastic as canoeist No. 1. "So you boys want to get canoes, do you?" said he. "Well, there is only one canoe for you to get, and that is the 'Shadow.' She paddles easily, and sails faster than any other canoe. She's not a flat-bottomed skiff, like the 'Rice Laker,' that will spill you whenever a squall strikes her, but she has good bearings, and you can't capsize her unless you try hard. Then, she is decked all over, and you can sleep in her at night, and keep dry even in a thunder-storm; her water-tight compartments have hatches in them, so that you can stow blankets and things in them that you want to keep dry; and she has a keel, so that when you run rapids, and she strikes on a rock, she will strike on her keel instead of her planks. It isn't worth while for you to look at any other canoe, for there is no canoe except the 'Shadow' that is worth having."

"You don't think much of the 'Rice Lake' canoe, then?" asked Harry.

"Why, she isn't a civilized canoe at all," replied the canoeist. "She is nothing but a heavy, wooden copy of the Indian birch. She hasn't any deck, she hasn't any water-tight compartments, and she hasn't any keel. Whatever else you do, don't get a 'Rice Laker.'"

The boys thanked the advocate of the "Shadow," and when they found themselves in the street again they wondered which of the two canoeists could be right, for each directly contradicted the other, and each seemed to be perfectly sincere. They reconsidered their decision to buy "Rice Lake" canoes, and looked forward with interest to their meeting with canoeist No. 3.

That gentleman was just as pleasant as the other two, but he did not agree with a single thing that they had said. "There are several different models of canoes," he remarked, "but that is simply because there are ignorant people in the world. Mr. Macgregor, the father of canoeing, always uses a 'Rob Roy' canoe, and no man who has once been in a good 'Rob Roy' will ever get into any other canoe. The 'Rob Roy' paddles like a feather, and will outsail any other canoe. She weighs twenty pounds less than those great, lumbering canal-boats, the 'Shadow' and the 'Rice Laker,' and it don't break your back to paddle her or to carry her round a dam. She is decked over, but her deck isn't all cut up with hatches. There's plenty of room to sleep in her, and her water-tight compartments are what they pretend to be—not a couple of leaky boxes stuffed full of blankets."

"We have been advised," began Charley, "to get 'Shadows' or 'Rice'—"

"Don't you do it," interrupted the canoeist. "It's lucky for you that you came to see me. It is a perfect shame for people to try to induce you to waste your money on worthless canoes. Mind you get

'Rob Roys,' and nothing else. Other canoes don't deserve the name. They are schooners, or scows, or canal-boats, but the 'Rob Roy' is a genuine canoe."

"Now for the last canoeist on the list!" exclaimed Harry as the boys left the office of canoeist No. 3. "I wonder what sort of a canoe he uses?"

"I'm glad there is only one more of them for us to see," said Joe. "The Commodore told us to believe all they said, and I'm trying my best to do it, but it's the hardest job I ever tried."

The fourth canoeist was, on the whole, the most courteous and amiable of the four. He begged his young friends to pay no attention to those who recommended wooden canoes, no matter what model they might be. "Canvas," said he, "is the only thing that a canoe should be built of. It is light and strong, and if you knock a hole in it you can mend it in five minutes. If you want to spend a great deal of money and own a yacht that is too small to sail in with comfort and too clumsy to be paddled, buy a wooden canoe; but if you really want to cruise, you will, of course, get canvas canoes."

"We have been advised to get 'Rice Lakers,' 'Shadows,' and 'Rob Roys,'" said Tom, "and we did not know until now that there was such a thing as a canvas canoe."

"It is very sad," replied the canoeist, "that people should take pleasure in giving such advice. They must know better. However, the subject is a painful one, and we won't discuss it. Take my advice, my dear boys, and get canvas canoes. All the really good canoeists in the country would say the same thing to you."

"We must try," said Joe, as the boys walked back to the Commodore's office, "to believe that the 'Rice Laker,' the 'Shadow,' the 'Rob Roy,' and the canvas canoe is the best one ever built. It seems to me something like believing that four and one are just the same. Perhaps you fellows can do it, but I'm not strong enough to believe as much as that all at one time."

The Commodore smiled when the boys entered his office for the second time and said, "Well, of course you've found out what is the best canoe, and know just what you want to buy?"

"We've seen four men," replied Harry, "and each one says that the canoe that he recommends is the only good one, and that all the others are good for nothing."

"I might have sent you to four other men, and they would have told you of four other canoes, each of which is the best in existence. But perhaps you have already heard enough to make up your minds."

"We're farther from making up our minds than ever," said Harry. "I do wish you would tell us what kind of canoe is really the best."

"The truth is," said the Commodore, "that there isn't much to choose among the different models of canoes, and you'll find that every canoeist is honestly certain that he has the best one. Now, I won't undertake to select canoes for you, though I will suggest that a light 'Rob Roy' would probably be a

A Decision Arrived At.

good choice for the smallest of you boys. Why don't you try all four of the canoes that have just been recommended to you? Then, if you cruise together, you can perhaps find out if any one of them is really better than the others. I will give you the names of three or four builders, all of whom build good, strong boats."

This advice pleased the boys, and they resolved to accept it. That evening they all met at Harry's home and decided what canoes they would get. Harry determined to get a "Shadow," Tom a "Rice Laker," Charley a canvas canoe, and Joe a "Rob Roy;" and the next morning orders for the four canoes were mailed to the builders whom the Commodore had recommended.

Chapter II.

IT was some time before the canoes were ready, and in the mean time the young canoeists met with a new difficulty. The canoe-builders wrote to them wishing to know how they would have the canoes rigged. It had never occurred to the boys that there was more than one rig used on canoes, and of course they did not know how to answer the builders' question. So they went to the Commodore and told him their difficulty.

"I might do," said he, "just as I did when I told you to go and ask four different canoeists which is the best canoe; but I won't put you to that trouble. I rather like the Lord Ross lateen rig better than any other, but, as you are going to try different kinds of canoes, it would be a good idea for you to try different rigs. For example, have your 'Rob Roy' rigged with lateen-sails; rig the 'Shadow' with a balance-lug, the 'Rice Laker' with a 'sharpie' leg-of-mutton, and the canvas canoe with the standing lug. Each one of these rigs has its advocates, who will prove to you that it is better than any other, and you can't do better than try them all. Only be sure to tell the builders that every canoe must have two masts, and neither of the two sails must be too big to be safely handled."

"How does it happen that every canoeist is so perfectly certain that he has the best canoe and the best rig in existence?" asked Tom.

"That is one of the great merits of canoeing," replied the Commodore. "It makes every man contented, and develops in him decision of character. I've known a canoeist to have a canoe so leaky that he spent half his time bailing her out, and rigged in such a way that she would neither sail nor do anything in a breeze except capsize; and yet he was never tired of boasting of the immense superiority of his canoe. There's a great deal of suffering in canoeing," continued the Commodore, musingly, " but its effects on the moral character are priceless. My dear boys, you have no idea how happy and contented you will be when you are wet through, cramped and blistered, and have to go into camp in a heavy rain, and without any supper except dry crackers."

While the boys were waiting for their canoes they read all the books on canoeing that they could find, and searched through a dozen volumes of the London *Field*, which they found in Uncle John's library, for articles and letters on canoeing. They thus learned a good deal, and when their canoes arrived they were able to discuss their respective merits with a good degree of intelligence.

The "Rob Roy" and the "Shadow" were built with white cedar planks and Spanish cedar decks. They shone with varnish, and their nickel-plated metal-work was as bright as silver. They were decidedly the prettiest of the four canoes, and it would have been very difficult to decide which was the prettier of the two. The "Rice Laker" was built without timbers or a keel, and was formed of two thicknesses of planking riveted together, the grain of the inner planking crossing that of the outer planking at right angles. She looked strong and serviceable, and before Tom had been in possession of her half an hour he was insisting that she was much the handiest canoe of the squadron, simply because she had no deck. The outside planks were of butternut; but they were pierced with so many rivets that they did not present so elegant an appearance as did the planks of the "Shadow" and the "Rob Roy." The canvas canoe consisted of a wooden skeleton-frame, covered and decked with painted canvas. She was very much the same in model as the "Shadow;" and though she seemed ugly in comparison with her varnished sisters, Charley claimed that he would get more comfort out of his canoe than the other boys would out of theirs, for the reason that scratches that would spoil the beauty of the varnished wood could not seriously injure the painted canvas. Thus each boy was quite contented, and asserted that he would not change canoes with anybody. They were equally well contented with the way in which their canoes were rigged, and they no longer wondered at the confident way in which the canoeists to whom the Commodore had introduced them spoke of the merits of their respective boats.

Of course the subject of names for the canoes had been settled long before the canoes arrived. Joe had named his "Rob Roy" the *Dawn;* Harry's canoe was the *Sunshine;* Tom's the *Twilight;* and Charley's the *Midnight.* The last name did not seem particularly appropriate to a canoe, but it was in keeping with the other names, and, as the canoe was painted black, it might have been supposed to have some reference to her color.

The boys had intended to join the American Canoe Association, but Uncle John suggested that they would do well to make a cruise, and to become real canoeists, before asking for admission to the association. They then decided to form a canoe club of their own, which they did; and Harry was elected the first Commodore of the Columbian Canoe Club, the flag of which was a pointed burgee of blue silk, with a white paddle worked upon it. Each canoe carried its private signal in addition to the club flag, and bore its name in gilt letters on a blue ground on each bow.

Where to cruise was a question which was decided and reconsidered half a dozen times. From the books which they had read the boys had learned that there is, if anything, more fun in cruising on a narrow stream than in sailing on broad rivers; that running rapids is a delightful sport, and that streams should always be descended instead of ascended in a canoe. They, therefore, wanted to discover a narrow stream with safe and easy rapids, and also to cruise on some lake or wide river where they could test the canoes under sail and under paddle in rough water. They learned more of the geography of the Eastern States and of Canada, in searching the map for a good cruising route, than they had ever learned at school; and they finally selected a route which seemed to combine all varieties of canoeing.

The cruise was to begin at the southern end of Lake Memphremagog, in Vermont. On this lake, which is thirty miles long, the young canoeists expected to spend several days, and to learn to handle the canoes under sail. From the northern end of the lake, which is in Canada, they intended to descend its outlet, the Magog River, which is a narrow stream, emptying into the St. Francis River at Sherbrooke. From Sherbrooke the St. Francis was to be descended to the St. Lawrence, down which the canoes were to sail to Quebec. They wrote to the post-master at Sherbrooke asking him if the Magog and the St. Francis were navigable by canoes, and when he replied that there were only one or two rapids in the Magog, which they could easily run, they were more then ever satisfied with their route.

The previous cruises that the boys had made had taught them what stores and provisions were absolutely necessary and what could be spared. Each canoe was provided with a water-proof bag to hold a blanket and dry clothes, and with a pair of small cushions stuffed with elastic felt, a material lighter than cork, and incapable of retaining moisture. These cushions were to be used as mattresses at night, and the rubber blankets were to be placed over the canoes and used as shelter tents. Although the mattresses would have made excellent life-preservers, Uncle John presented each canoeist with a rubber life-belt, which could be buckled around the waist in a few seconds in case of danger of a capsize. Harry provided his canoe with a canvas canoe-tent, made from drawings published in the London *Field*, but the others decided not to go to the expense of making similar tents until Harry's should have been thoroughly tested.

When all was ready the blankets and stores were packed in the *Sunshine*, the cockpit of which was provided with hatches, which could be locked up, thus making the canoe serve the purpose of a trunk. The four canoes were then sent by rail to Newport, at the southern end of Lake Memphremagog, and a week later the boys followed them, carrying their paddles by hand, for the reason that, if they had been sent with the canoes and had been lost or stolen, it would have been impossible to start on the cruise until new paddles had been procured.

Newport was reached, after an all-night journey, at about two o'clock in the morning. The canoeists went straight to the freight-house to inspect the canoes. They were all there, resting on the heads of a long row of barrels, and were apparently all right. The varnish of the *Dawn* and the *Sunshine* was scratched in a few places, and the canvas canoe had a very small hole punched through her deck, as if she had been too intimate with a nail in the course of her journey. The boys were, however, well satisfied with the appearance of the boats, and so walked up to the hotel to get dinner and a supply of sandwiches, bread, and eggs for their supper.

Dinner was all ready, for, under the name of breakfast, it was waiting for the passengers of the train, which made a stop of half an hour at Newport. A band was playing on the deck of a steamer which was just about to start down the lake, and the boys displayed appetites, as they sat near the open window looking out on the beautiful landscape, which rather astonished the waiter.

A good, quiet place for launching the canoes was found, which was both shady and out of sight of the hotel. It was easy enough to carry the three empty canoes down to the shore; but the *Sunshine*, with her heavy cargo, proved too great a load, and about half-way between the freight-house and the shore she had to be laid on the ground and partly emptied. Here Joe, who tried to carry the spars and paddles of four canoes on his shoulder, found that there is nothing more exasperating than a load of sticks of different sizes. No matter how firmly he tried to hold them together, they would spread apart at every imaginable angle. Before he had gone three rods he looked like some new kind of porcupine with gigantic quills sticking out all over him. Then he began to drop things, and, stooping to pick them up, managed to trip himself and fall with a tremendous clatter. He picked himself up and made sixteen journeys between the spot where he fell and the shore of the lake, carrying only one spar at a time, and grasping that with both hands. His companions sat down on the grass and laughed to see the deliberate way in which he made his successive journeys, but Joe, with a perfectly serious face, said that he was going to get the better of those spars, no matter how much trouble it might cost him, and that he was not going to allow them to get together and play tricks on him again.

It was tiresome stooping over, packing the canoes, but finally they were all in order, and the Commodore gave the order to launch them. The lake was perfectly calm, and the little fleet started under

"SHE'S HALF FULL OF WATER."

paddle for a long, sandy point that jutted out into the lake some three miles from Newport. The *Sunshine* and the *Dawn* paddled side by side, and the two other canoes followed close behind them.

"Boys, isn't this perfectly elegant?" exclaimed Harry, laying down his paddle when the fleet was about a mile from the shore and bathing his hot head with water from the lake. "Did you ever see anything so lovely as this blue water?"

"Yes," said Charley; "the water's all right outside of the canoes, but I'd rather have a little less inside of mine."

"What do you mean," asked Harry. "Is she leaking?"

"She's half full of water, that's all," replied Charley, beginning to bail vigorously with his hat.

"Halloo!" cried Joe, suddenly. "Here's the water up to the top of my cushions."

"We'd better paddle on and get ashore as soon as possible," said Harry. "My boat is leaking a little too."

Charley bailed steadily for ten minutes, and somewhat reduced the amount of water in his canoe. The moment he began paddling, however, the leak increased. He paddled with his utmost strength, knowing that if he did not soon reach land he would be swamped; but the water-logged canoe was very heavy, and he could not drive her rapidly through the water. His companions kept near him, and advised him to drop his paddle and to bail, but he knew that the water was coming in faster than he could bail it out, and so he wasted no time in the effort. It soon became evident that his canoe would never keep afloat to reach the sand spit for which he had been steering, so he turned aside and paddled for a little clump of rushes, where he knew the water must be shallow. Suddenly he stopped paddling, and almost at the same moment his canoe sunk under him, and he sprung up to swim clear of her.

Chapter III.

LUCKILY the water was only four feet deep, as Charley found when he tried to touch bottom; so he stopped swimming, and, with the water nearly up to his shoulders, stood still and began to think what to do next.

The canoes—including the sunken *Midnight*—were a good mile from the shore, and although the sandy shoal on which Charley was standing was firm and hard it was of small extent, and the water all around it was too deep to be waded.

"You'll have to get into one of our canoes," said Harry.

"How am I going to do it without capsizing her?" replied Charley.

"I don't believe it can be done," said Harry, as he

looked first at the *Sunshine* and then at the *Twilight;* "but then you've got to do it somehow. You can't swim a whole mile, can you?"

"Of course I can't, but then it wouldn't do me any good to spill one of you fellows by trying to climb out of the water into a canoe that's as full now as she ought to be. Besides, I'm not going to desert the *Midnight.*"

"I thought the *Midnight* had deserted you," said Joe. "If my canoe should go to the bottom of the lake without giving me any warning, I shouldn't think it a bit rude to leave her there."

"Don't talk nonsense!" exclaimed Charley; "but come here and help me get my canoe afloat again. We can do it, I think, if we go to work the right way."

Charley found no difficulty in getting hold of the painter of his canoe with the help of his paddle. Giving the end of the painter to Joe, he took the *Dawn's* painter, and by ducking down under the water succeeded after two or three attempts in reeving it through the stern-post of the sunken canoe, and giving one end to Harry and the other to Tom. Then, taking the bow painter from Joe, he grasped it firmly with both hands, and at a given signal all the boys, except Joe, made a desperate effort to bring the wreck to the surface.

They could not do it. They managed to raise her off the bottom, but Harry and Tom in their canoes could not lift to any advantage, and so were forced to let her settle down again.

"I've got to unload her," said Charley, gloomily. "I think we can get her up if there is nothing in her except water. Anyhow we've got to try."

It was tiresome work to get the water-soaked stores and canned provisions out of the canoe, and Charley had to duck his head under the water at least a dozen times before the heaviest part of the *Midnight's* cargo could be brought up and passed into the other canoes. His comrades wanted to jump overboard and help him, but he convinced them that they would have great difficulty in climbing back into their canoes, and that in all probability they would capsize themselves in so doing. "He's right!" cried Joe. "Commodore, please make an order that hereafter only one canoe shall be wrecked at a time. We must keep some dry stores in the fleet."

When the *Midnight* was partly unloaded a new and successful effort was made to raise her. As soon as she reached the surface Charley rolled her over, bottom upward, and in this position the small amount of air imprisoned under her kept her afloat.

The cause of the leak was quickly discovered. There was a hole through her canvas bottom nearly an inch in diameter, made by some blow she had received while on the way to the lake. The wonder was, not that she sunk when she did, but that she had floated long enough to be paddled a mile. It is probable that the ballast-bag, which was close by the hole, had partly stopped the leak at first, but had afterward been slightly moved, thus permitting the water to rush freely in.

The surface of painted canvas dries very quickly

in the hot sun, and it was not long before the bottom of the *Midnight* was dry enough to be temporarily patched. Harry lighted his spirit-lamp and melted a little of the lump of rosin and tallow which had been provided for mending leaks. This was spread over a patch of new canvas: the patch was then placed over the hole, and more of the melted rosin and tallow smeared over it. In about fifteen minutes the patch was dry enough to be serviceable, and Charley righted the canoe, bailed her out, and by throwing himself across the cockpit, and then carefully turning himself so as to get his legs into it, found himself once more afloat and ready to paddle.

The canoe still leaked, but the leak could be kept under without difficulty by occasional bailing, and in the course of half an hour the sand-spit for which the fleet had started was reached. It was part of a large island with steep, rocky shores and a beautiful little sandy beach. It was just the place for a camp; and though the boys had expected to camp some miles farther north, the sinking of Charley's canoe had so delayed them that it was already nearly six o'clock, and they therefore decided to paddle no farther that day.

The canoes were hauled out on the beach, and unloaded and shored up with their rudders, backboards, and a few pieces of drift-wood so as to stand on an even keel. Then came the work of rigging shelters over them for the night. Harry's canoe-tent was supported by four small upright sticks resting on the deck and fitting into cross-pieces sewed into the roof of the tent. The sides and ends buttoned down to the gunwale and deck of the canoe, and two curtains, one on each side, which could be rolled up like carriage-curtains in fair weather and buttoned down in rainy weather, served both as the doors and windows of the tent. The shelters rigged by the other boys were much less complete. The two masts of each canoe were stepped, the paddle was lashed between them, and a rubber blanket was hung over the paddle, with its edges reaching nearly to the ground. The blankets and the bags which served as pillows were then arranged, and the canoes were ready for the night.

It was a warm and clear night, and a breeze which came up from the south at sunset blew the mosquitoes away. Harry found his tent, with the curtains rolled up, cool and pleasant; but his fellow-canoeists found themselves fairly suffocating under their rubber blankets, and were compelled to throw them aside.

Toward morning, when the day was just beginning to dawn, the canoeists were suddenly awakened by a rush of many heavy, trampling feet which shook the ground. It was enough to startle any one, and the boys sprung up in such a hurry that Harry struck his head against the roof of his tent, knocked it down, upset the canoe, and could not at first decide whether he was taking part in a railway collision or whether an earthquake of the very best quality had happened. The cause of the disturbance was a herd of horses trotting down to the water's edge to drink. There were at least twenty of them, and had the canoes happened to be in their path they might have stumbled over them in the faint morning light; in which case the boys would have had the experience of being shipwrecked on dry land.

A gentle southerly breeze wrinkled the water while breakfast was cooking, and the Commodore ordered that the masts and sails should be got ready for use. It was impossible to make an early start, for Charley's blankets had to be dried in the sun, and the hole in his canoe had to be repaired with a new patch in a thorough and workmanlike way. It was, therefore, ten o'clock before the canoes were ready to be launched; and in the mean time the wind had increased so much that the boys decided to use only their main-sails.

The moment the sails drew the canoes shot off at a pace which filled the young canoeists with delight. The canoes were in good trim for sailing, as they were not overloaded; and while they were skirting the west shore of the island the water was quite smooth. Each canoe carried a bag partly filled with sand for ballast, and every one except Joe had lashed his ballast-bag to the keelson. This was a precaution which Joe had forgotten to take, and before long he had good reason to regret his error.

As soon as the northern end of the island was passed the canoes came to a part of the lake where there was quite a heavy sea. The *Dawn* and the *Twilight* were steered by the paddle, which passed through a row-lock provided for the purpose; and Joe and Tom found little difficulty in keeping their canoes directly before the wind. The two other canoes were steered with rudders, and occasionally, when their bows dipped, their rudders were thrown nearly out of the water, in consequence of which they steered wildly. All the canoes showed a tendency to roll a good deal, and now and then a little water would wash over the deck. It was fine sport running down the lake with such a breeze, and the boys enjoyed it immensely.

The wind continued to rise, and the lake became

covered with white caps. "Commodore," said Charley Smith, "I don't mean to show any disrespect to my commanding officer, but it seems to me this is getting a little risky."

"How is it risky?" asked Harry. "You're a sailor and know twice as much about boats as I do, if I am Commodore."

"It's risky in two or three ways. For instance, if the wind blows like this much longer a following sea will swamp some one of us."

"Oh! we're going fast enough to keep out of the way of the sea," cried Joe.

"Just notice how your canoe comes almost to a dead stop every time she sinks between two seas, and you won't feel quite so sure that you're running faster than the sea is."

The boys saw that Charley was right. The canoes were so light that they lost their headway between the seas, and it was evident that they were in danger of being overtaken by a following sea.

"Tell us two or three more dangers, just to cheer

us up, won't you?" asked Joe, who was in high spirits with the excitement of the sail.

"There's the danger of rolling our booms under, and there is a great deal of danger that Harry's canoe and mine will broach-to when our rudders are out of water."

"What will happen if they do broach-to?"

"They'll capsize, that's all," replied Charley.

"What had we better do?" asked Harry. "There's no use in capsizing ourselves in the middle of the lake."

"My advice is that we haul on the port tack, and run over to the west shore. The moment we get this wind and sea on the quarter we shall be all right — though, to be sure, we've got more sail up than we ought to have."

The canoes were quite near together, with the exception of the *Twilight*, which was outsailing the others; but even she was still near enough to be hailed. Harry hailed her, and ordered the fleet to steer for a cove on the west shore. As soon as the wind was brought on the port quarter the canoes increased their speed; and although the *Twilight* made more leeway than the others, she drew ahead of them very fast. The wind was now precisely what the canoes wanted to bring out their sailing qualities. The *Sunshine* soon showed that she was the most weatherly, as the *Twilight* was the least weatherly, of the fleet. The *Midnight* kept up very fairly with the *Sunshine;* and the *Dawn*, with her small lateen-sail, skimmed over the water so fast that it was evident that if she could have carried the big balance-lug of the *Sunshine* she would easily have beaten her.

The canoes were no longer in danger of being swamped; but the wind continuing to rise, the boys found that they were carrying more sail than was safe. They did not want to take in their sails and paddle, and though all of the sails except the *Dawn's* lateen could be reefed, nobody wanted to be the first to propose to reef; and Harry, in his excitement, forgot all about reefing. The wind, which had been blowing very steadily, now began to blow in gusts, and the boys had to lean far out to windward to keep their canoes right side up.

"We can't keep on this way much longer without coming to grief," Charley cried at the top of his lungs, so that Harry, who was some distance to windward, could hear him.

"What do you say?" replied Harry.

"We've got too much sail on," yelled Charley.

"Of course we'll sail on. This is perfectly gorgeous!" was Harry's answer.

"He don't hear," said Charley. "I say, Joe, you'd better take in your main-sail, and set the dandy in its place. You'll spill yourself presently."

"The dandy's stowed down below, where I can't get at it. I guess I can hold her up till we get across."

Tom was by this time far out of hailing distance, and was apparently getting on very well. Charley did not doubt that he could manage his own canoe well enough, but he was very uneasy about Harry and Joe, who did not seem to realize that they were carrying sail altogether too recklessly. The fleet was nearly two miles from the shore, and a capsize in the heavy sea that was running would have been no joke.

Charley turned part way around in his canoe to see if his life-belt was in handy reach. As he did so he saw that the water a quarter of a mile to windward was black with a fierce squall that was approaching. He instantly brought his canoe up to the wind, so that the squall would strike him on the port bow, and called out to Harry and Joe to follow his example. Harry did not hear him, and Joe, instead of promptly following Charley's advice, stopped to wonder what he was trying to do. The squall explained the matter almost immediately. It struck the *Sunshine* and the *Dawn*, and instantly capsized them, and then rushed on to overtake Tom, and to convince him that Lake Memphremagog is not a good place for inexperienced canoeists who want to carry sail recklessly in squally weather.

Chapter IV.

FROM the books they had read Harry and Joe had learned exactly what to do in case of capsizing under sail, and had often discussed the matter. "When I capsize," Harry would say, "I shall pull the masts out of her, and she'll then right of her own accord. Then I shall unship the rudder, put my hands on the stern-post, and raise myself up so that I can straddle the deck, and gradually work my way along until I can get into the cockpit. After that I shall bail her out, step the masts, and sail on again." Nothing could be easier than to describe this plan while sitting in a comfortable room on shore, but to carry it out in a rough sea was a different affair.

Harry was not at all frightened when he found himself in the water, and he instantly swum clear of the canoe, to avoid becoming entangled in her rigging. He then proceeded to unship the masts and the rudder, and when this was done tried to climb in over the stern. He found that it was quite impossible. No sooner would he get astride of the stern than the canoe would roll and throw him into the water again. After half a dozen attempts he gave it up, and swimming to the side of the canoe managed to throw himself across the cockpit. This was the way in which Charley Smith had climbed into his canoe the day before, and to Harry's great surprise —for no such method of climbing into a canoe had been mentioned in any of the books he had read—it proved successful

Of course the deck of the canoe was now level with the water, which washed in and out of her with every sea that struck her. Harry seized the empty tin can which he used as a bailer, and which was made fast to one of the timbers of the canoe with a line, to prevent it from floating away, but he could not make any headway in bailing her out.

The water washed into her just as fast as he could throw it out again, and he began to think that he should have to paddle the canoe ashore full of water. This would have been hard work, for with so much water in her she was tremendously heavy and unwieldy; but, after getting her head up to the wind with his paddle, he found that less water washed into her, and after long and steady work he succeeded in bailing most of it out.

Meanwhile Charley, whose help Harry had declined, because he felt so sure that he could get out of his difficulty by following the plan that he had learned from books on canoeing, was trying to help Joe. At first Joe thought it was a good joke to be capsized. His Lord Ross lateen-sail, with its boom and yard, had floated clear of the canoe of its own accord, and, as the only spar left standing was a mast about two feet high, she ought to have righted. But Joe had forgotten to lash his sand-bag to the keelson, and the result was that whenever he touched the canoe she would roll completely over and come

paddle are joined together by a ferrule in the middle
—he could paddle against a head-wind with much
less labor.

The *Twilight*, being an undecked "Rice Lake" canoe, could easily carry two persons, and, with the help of Charley and Tom, Joe climbed into her. Charley then picked up the floating sail of the *Dawn*, made her painter fast to his own stern, and started under paddle for the shore. It was not a light task to tow the water-logged canoe, but both the sea and the wind helped him, and he landed by the time that the other boys had got the camp-fire started and the coffee nearly ready.

"Well," said Harry, "I've learned how to get into a canoe to-day. If I'd stuck to the rule and tried to get in over the stern I should be out in the lake yet."

"I'm going to write to the London *Field* and get it to print my new rule about capsizing," said Joe.

"What's that?" asked Charley. "To turn somersaults in the water? That was what you were doing all the time until Tom came up."

"That was for exercise, and had nothing to do with my rule, which is, 'Always have a fellow in a "Rice Lake" canoe to pick you up.'"

"All your trouble came from forgetting to lash your ballast-bag," remarked Harry. "I hope it will teach you a lesson."

"That's a proper remark for a Commodore who wants to enforce discipline," cried Charley; "but I insist that the trouble came from carrying too much sail."

"The sail would have been all right if it hadn't been for the wind," replied Harry.

"And the wind wouldn't have done us any harm if we hadn't been on the lake," added Joe.

"Boys, attention!" cried Harry. "Captain Charles Smith is hereby appointed sailing-master of this fleet, and will be obeyed and respected accordingly, or, at any rate, as much as he can make us obey and respect him. Anyhow, it will be his duty to tell us how much sail to carry, and how to manage the canoes under sail."

"What will we do for blankets? It's too cold to sleep without them."

"We can each borrow one from Harry and Charley. They've got two apiece, and can spare one of them."

Joe's plan was evidently the only one to be adopted; and so the two boys pitched their little rubber tent, borrowed two blankets, and crept under shelter. They were decidedly wet, but they lay close together and managed to keep warm. In the morning they woke up rested and comfortable, to find a bright sun shining and their clothes dried by the heat of their bodies. Neither had taken the slightest cold, although they had run what was undoubtedly a serious risk, in spite of the fact that one does not easily take cold when camping out.

As they were enjoying their breakfast the canoeists naturally talked over the events of the previous day and night. Harry had been kept perfectly dry by his canoe tent—one side of which he had left open, so as to have plenty of fresh air; and Charley had also been well protected from the rain by his rubber blanket, hung in the usual way over the paddle, although he had been far too warm to be comfortable.

"I'm tired of suffocating under that rubber blanket of mine, and I've invented a new way of covering the canoe at night, which will leave me a little air to breathe. I'll explain it to you when we camp to-night, Joe."

"I'm glad to hear it, for I've made up my mind that I'd rather be rained on than take a Turkish bath all night long under that suffocating blanket."

"Will your new plan work on my canoe?" asked Tom.

"No; nothing will keep that 'Rice Lake' bath-tub of yours dry in a rain, unless you deck her over."

"That's what I'm going to do when we get to Magog. I'll buy some canvas and deck over the ends of my canoe. Sleeping in her in the rain as she is now is like sleeping in a cistern with the water running into it."

"Now that we've had a chance to try our sails, which rig do you like best, Sailing-master?" asked Harry.

"That lateen-rig that Joe has," replied Charley. "He can set his sail and take it in while the rest of us are trying to find our halyards. Did you see how the whole concern—spars and sail—floated free of the canoe of their own accord the moment she capsized?"

"That's so; but then my big balance-lug holds more wind than Joe's sail."

"It held too much yesterday. It's a first-rate rig for racing, but it isn't anything like as handy as the lateen for cruising; neither is my standing-lug. I tried to get it down in a hurry yesterday, and the halyards jammed, and I couldn't get it down for two or three minutes."

"I can get my leg-of-mutton in easy enough," remarked Tom, "but I can't get the mast out of the step unless the water's perfectly smooth, and I don't believe I could then without going ashore."

"Now, Commodore," said Charley, "if you'll give the order to start, I'll give the order to carry all sail. The breeze is light and the water is smooth, and we ought to run down to the end of the lake by noon."

The little fleet made a beautiful appearance as it cruised down the lake under full sail. The breeze was westerly, which fact enabled the canoes to carry their after-sails—technically known as "dandies"—to much advantage. When running directly before the wind the "dandy" is sometimes a dangerous sail, as it is apt to make the canoe broach-to; but with a wind from any other direction than dead aft it is a very useful sail.

The canoes sailed faster than they had sailed the day before, because there was no rough sea to check their headway. They reached Magog at noon, went to the hotel for a good dinner, bought some canvas with which to deck Tom's canoe, and then looked at the dam which crosses the Magog River a few rods from the lake, and wondered how they were ever to get through the rapids below it.

There was a place where the canoes could be lowered one by one over the breast of the dam and launched in a little eddy immediately below. The rapids, which extended from below the dam for nearly a quarter of a mile, were, however, very uninviting to a timid canoeist. The water did not seem to be more than three or four feet deep, but it was very swift, and full of rocks. "You boys can't never run them rapids in them boats," said a man who came to look at the canoes. "You'll have to get a cart and haul round 'em."

The boys did not like to be daunted by their first rapid, and, as there did not seem to be much risk of drowning, they decided to take the chances of getting the canoes through it safely. Harry gave the order to lash everything fast in the canoes that could be washed overboard, and he prepared to lead the way in the *Sunshine*.

It was magnificent sport shooting down the rapid like an arrow. The canoes drove through two or three waves which washed the decks, though the canoe-aprons of the *Dawn, Sunshine,* and *Midnight* kept the water from getting into the cockpits. Harry's and Charley's canoes each struck once on the same rock while in the rapid, but in each case only the keel struck the rock, and the current dragged the canoes safely over it. When the fleet was reunited in the smooth water below the rapid the boys expressed their enthusiasm by all talking at once at the top of their lungs. Every one was delighted with the way his canoe had acted, and with the skill with which he had avoided this or that rock, or had discovered the best channel just at the right moment. In their excitement they let the canoes float gently down the stream, until they suddenly discovered another rapid at the beginning of a sharp bend in the river just ahead of them.

It was nothing like as fierce in appearance as the first rapid, and as Harry led the way the others followed close after him, one behind the other, fancying that they could run the rapid without the least trouble. Half-way down Harry's canoe struck on a rock, swung broadside to the current, and hung there. Tom was so close behind him that he could not alter his course, and so ran straight into the *Sunshine* with a terrible crash. The *Dawn* and the *Twilight* instantly followed, and as the four canoes thus piled together keeled over and spilled their occupants into the river, it began to look as if the rapid had determined to make the irreverent young canoeists respect it.

Chapter V.

WHEN the boys were compelled to jump overboard they could see that the water was only about two feet deep; but they did not know whether they could stand up against the fierce current. They found that they could, although they had to move slowly to avoid being swept off their feet. Harry's canoe was easily pushed off the rock on which it had run, and the moment it was out of the way the other canoes were free. Each canoeist seized the stern of his own canoe, and let it drag him down the rest of the rapid, which fortunately was a short one. While performing this feat the knees of the canoeists were scraped over the rocks, and they received several unpleasant bruises; but they thought it was impossible to get into their canoes in swift water, and so had no choice except to float down hanging on to the sterns of the canoes.

Reaching the smooth water, they swum and pushed the canoes before them toward the shore. Here they found a great bank of sawdust that had floated down the river from the mill at Magog, and it was so soft and elastic that they determined to sleep on it that night, instead of sleeping in their canoes, since the sky was perfectly clear and there was no danger of rain.

The canoes were hauled out on the bank, so that the stores could be readily taken out of them. The canvas canoe did not seem to be in the least injured either by the rock on which she had struck or by the collision with the other canoes. Harry's canoe had sustained a little damage where one of the planks had been ground against the rock on which she had hung so long, but it was not enough to cause her to leak, and the injuries of the other canoes were confined to their varnish.

"All the trouble," remarked Harry, "came from

following too close after one another. To-morrow, if we find any more rapids, we will keep the canoes far enough apart, so that if one canoe runs aground the others can turn out for her."

"We could have got into the canoes easy enough if we had only thought so," said Tom. "If I'd stood up on the rock and held the canoe along-side of it, I could have stepped in without any difficulty."

"Why didn't you do it, then?" asked Harry.

"Because I didn't happen to think of it, and because all the rest of you had started to float down after your canoes."

"I noticed one thing about a rapid which if I was Commodore it would be my duty to impress on your faithful but ignorant minds," said Joe. "When you see a big ripple on the water the rock that makes it isn't under the ripple, but is about four or five feet higher up stream."

"That's so!" exclaimed Harry. "I ought to have remembered that, for Macgregor speaks about it in one of his books."

"Whereabouts did your canoe strike, Commodore?" inquired Charley.

"Oh, about midships."

"And of course she swung round broadside to the current."

"Didn't she, though! If I'd jumped out of her on the side I intended to when she first struck she would have swung against my legs; but I remembered that you must always jump out of a canoe in a rapid on the side above her."

"What do you mean by the side above her?" asked Tom.

"I mean that you must not jump out below her."

"That's as clear as anything could be," said Joe. "Still, I'd like to know what you mean by 'below her.'"

"There's an upper end and a lower end to every rapid, isn't there?"

"Yes."

"Well, the side of the canoe toward the upper end of a rapid is what I call 'above her.' If you jump out on that side she can't float against your legs and smash them."

"Now, if you've got through with that question," continued Charley, "I want to say that if the Commodore had put his stores and his ballast-bag in the stern of his canoe, so as to make her draw a good deal more water aft than she did forward, she would have struck aft of midships, and wouldn't have swung around."

"You're right. That's just what Macgregor recommends, but I forgot it. Boys, I hereby order every canoe to be loaded with all her ballast and cargo in the after compartment before we start tomorrow."

"And I want to remind you fellows of one more thing," said Charley, "When the current is sweeping you toward a concave shore—that is, where the river makes a bend—don't try to keep your canoe clear of the shore by hard paddling. Just backwater on the side of the canoe that is toward the middle of the river."

"That's Macgregor again!" cried Harry; "but I'd forgotten it. To-morrow we'll run our rapids in real scientific style."

"Provided there are any more rapids," suggested Tom.

"What did that Sherbrooke postmaster say about the Magog rapids?" inquired Joe.

"Said there weren't any, except one or two which we could easily run," replied Harry.

"Then we've probably got through with the rapids," said Charley. "I'm rather sorry, for it's good fun running them."

Supper was now over, and the canoeists, spreading their rubber blankets on the sawdust, prepared to "turn in." They were in a wild and beautiful spot. The great "Rock Forest," as it is called, through which the Magog runs, is of vast extent and is inhabited by bears and smaller wild animals. The boys from their camping ground could see nothing but the river, the dense woods on either bank, and the bright moonlit sky above them. The rapid was roaring as if it was angry at having failed to wreck the canoes, and the only other sound was the crackling of branches in the forest, and the occasional sighing of the gentle breeze. The boys were tired, and, lulled by the sound of the rapids, soon dropped asleep.

The recent rains had dampened the sawdust to the depth of about two inches, but below this depth it was dry and inflammable. A small fire had been made with which to cook supper, and the dampness of the sawdust had made the boys so confident that the fire would not spread, that they had not taken the trouble to put it out before going to sleep.

Now, it happened that the damp sawdust on which the fire had been kindled gradually became dry, and finally took fire. It burnt very slowly on the surface, but the dry sawdust immediately below burnt like tinder. About two hours after Harry had closed his eyes he was awakened from a dream that he had upset a burning spirit-lamp over his legs. To his horror he saw that the whole bank of sawdust was on fire. Smoke was everywhere creeping up through the damp top layer, and at a little distance from the canoes the smouldering fire had burst into roaring flames.

Harry instantly called his comrades, and starting up they rushed to the canoes, threw their blankets and stores into them, and prepared to launch them. They had not a moment to spare. The flames were close to them, and were spreading every moment, and as they shoved the canoes toward the water their feet repeatedly sunk down through the ashes below the surface, the flames springing up as they hurriedly drew their feet back. It did not take many minutes to get the canoes into the water and to embark, but as the canoeists pushed out into the river the part of the bank where they had been sleeping burst into flames.

A light breeze had sprung up which was just enough to fan the fire and to carry it into an immense pile of dry driftwood that lay on the shore below the sawdust bank. The boys waited in the quiet eddy near the bank and watched the progress of the fire. It licked up the drift-wood in a very few moments, and then, roaring with exultation over the work it had done, it swept into the forest. In half an hour's time a forest fire was burning which threatened to make a terrible destruction of timber, and the heat had grown so intense that the canoeists were compelled to drop down the stream to avoid it.

Canoeing at night is always a ticklish business, but on a swift river, full of rapids, as is the Magog, it is exceedingly dangerous. The fire lighted the way for the fleet for a short distance, but before a landing-place was reached a turn on the river shut out the light, and at the same time the noise of a rapid close at hand was heard.

The boys had no desire to entangle themselves in unknown rapids in the dark, and paddled at once for the shore opposite to that where the fire was raging. They found when they reached it that it was a perpendicular bank on which it was impossible to land. They floated down a short distance,

"HE CAUGHT HOLD OF THE ROOT OF A TREE AND KEPT HIS CANOE STATIONARY."

hoping to find a landing spot, but none could be found. Then they attempted to cross the stream to the other shore, hoping that the fire would not spread in that direction. To their dismay they found that they were already almost within the clutch of the rapid. The current had become strong and swift, and it was evident before they had got half-way across the river that nothing but the hardest paddling could keep them from being drawn into the rapid. It was an occasion when everybody had to look out for himself and depend on his own paddles for safety. The young canoeists struck out manfully. Harry was the first to reach the shore, where he caught hold of the root of a tree and kept his canoe stationary. Tom followed closely behind him, and Harry told him to catch hold of the *Sunshine* until he could make the *Twilight's* painter fast to the root. Joe arrived a little later, for his canoe had run on a rock, and for a few minutes he was in great danger of a capsize.

The three canoeists succeeded in tying up to the

bank, where they expected every moment to be joined by Charley. The minutes passed on, but Charley did not appear. His comrades shouted for him, but there was no answer. Indeed, the rapid made such a noise, now that they were close upon it, that they could not have heard Charley's voice had he been a few yards from them.

The fear that an accident had happened to Charley made the other boys very uneasy. Joe cast his canoe loose and paddled out into the river and nearly across it, looking for some signs of the *Midnight* and her owner, but he came back unsuccessful, after having narrowly escaped being carried down the rapid. There could no longer be any doubt that the current had swept the *Midnight* away, and that Charley had been compelled to make the hazardous and almost hopeless attempt of running the rapid in the dark.

As soon as Joe returned Harry said that he would paddle out into the middle of the river where Charley was last seen, and would let his canoe drift down the rapid, but Tom and Joe insisted that he should do no such thing. Said Joe, " Either Charley is drowned or he isn't. If he isn't drowned he is somewhere at the foot of the rapid, where we'll find him as soon as it gets light. If he is drowned it won't do him any good for another of us to get drowned."

"Joe is right," said Tom. "We must stay here till daylight."

"And meanwhile Charley may be drowned!" exclaimed Harry.

"I don't believe he is," replied Tom. "He's the best canoeist of any of us, and he is too good a sailor to get frightened. Then, he is very cautious, and I'll bet that the first thing he did when he found himself in the rapid was to buckle his life-belt round him."

"If he did that it wouldn't hurt him if he were capsized."

"Not if the rapid is like those we've run, and the chances are that it is. I feel sure that Charley has got through it all right, and without losing his canoe. We'll find him waiting for us in the morning."

What Tom said seemed so reasonable that Harry

gave up his wild idea of running the rapid, and agreed to wait until daylight. It was already nearly one o'clock, and at that time of year the day began to dawn by half-past three. There was no opportunity for the boys to sleep, but they occasionally nodded as they sat in their canoes. About two o'clock Harry poked Tom with his paddle, and in a low voice called his attention to the crackling of the twigs in the woods a short distance from the bank. Something was evidently making its way through the forest and coming nearer every minute to the canoes. The boys grasped their pistols and anxiously waited. They remembered that there were bears in the woods, and they fully believed that one was on its way down to the water. "Don't fire," whispered Harry, "till I give the word;" but while he was speaking a dark form parted the underbrush on the bank above them and came out into full view.

Chapter VI.

THE early morning visitor was not a bear. He was a very welcome visitor, for as soon as he made himself visible he was seen to be the missing canoeist. Charley was very wet and cold, but he was soon furnished with dry clothes and a blanket, and warmed with a cup of hot coffee made with the help of Harry's spirit-lamp; and as he lay on the bank and waited for daylight he told the story of his midnight run down the rapid.

When the boys were crossing the river above the rapid Charley's canoe was close behind Joe's. The latter ran on a rock, and in order to avoid her Charley was compelled to pass below the rock. In so doing he found himself in great danger of running on another rock, and in his effort to avoid this he drifted still farther down the river. Before he was aware of his danger he was caught by the current at the head of the rapid. He had just time to turn his canoe so as to head her down stream and to buckle his life-belt around him. In another second he was rushing down the rapid at a rate that, in view of the darkness, was really frightful.

It was useless to attempt to guide the canoe. Charley could see so little in advance of him that he could not choose his channel nor avoid any rock that might lie in his path. He, therefore, sat still, trusting that the current would carry him into the deepest channel and keep him clear of the rocks. The rapid seemed to be a very long one, but the *Midnight* ran it without taking in a drop of water or striking a single rock.

As soon as quiet water was reached Charley paddled to the shore, intending to make his canoe fast and to sleep quietly in her until morning. He was in high spirits at having successfully run a rapid in the dark, and he paddled so carelessly that just as he was within a yard of the shore the canoe ran upon a sunken log, spilled her captain into the water, and then floated off in the darkness and disappeared.

Charley had no difficulty in getting ashore, but he was wet to the skin, and his dry clothes and all his property, except his paddle, had gone on a cruise without him. There was nothing for him to do but to make his way back along the bank to the other boys. This proved to be a tiresome task. The woods were very thick, and full of underbrush and fallen trunks. Charley was terribly scratched, and his clothes badly torn, as he slowly forced his way through the bushes and among the trees. He was beginning to think that he would never reach the boys, when he fortunately heard their voices as they whispered together.

When morning dawned the canoeists, feeling extremely cramped and stiff, cast their canoes loose, and started down the river, intending, if possible, to find Charley's canoe, and then go ashore for breakfast and a good long sleep. The rapid had been run so easily by Charley in the night that they rightly imagined they would find no difficulty in running it by daylight. Tom took Charley in the *Twilight*, and the fleet, with Harry leading the way, passed through the rapid without accident. The boys could not but wonder how Charley had escaped the rocks in the darkness, for the rapid, which was much the roughest and swiftest they had yet seen, seemed to be full of rocks.

Not very far below the rapid the missing canoe was discovered aground in an eddy. She was uninjured; and as there was a sandy beach and plenty of shade near at hand the boys went ashore, made their breakfast, and, lying down on their rubber blankets, slept until the afternoon.

It was time for dinner when the tired canoeists awoke, and by the time they had finished their meal and were once more afloat it was nearly three o'clock. They ran three more rapids without any trouble. Their canoes frequently struck on sunken rocks; but as they were loaded so as to draw more water aft

RUNNING THE RAPID.

than they did forward, they usually struck aft of midships, and did not swing around broadside to the current. When a canoe struck in this way her captain unjointed his paddle, and, taking a blade in each hand, generally succeeded in lifting her clear of the rock by pushing with both blades against the bottom of the river. In the next rapid Joe's canoe ran so high on a rock that was in the full force of the current that he could not get her afloat without getting out of her. He succeeded in getting into her again, however, without difficulty, by bringing her alongside of the rock on which he was standing, although he had to step in very quickly, as the current swept her away the moment he ceased to hold her.

In running these rapids the canoes were kept at a safe distance apart, so that when one ran aground the one following her had time to steer clear of her. At Charley's suggestion the painter of each canoe was rove through the stern-post instead of the stem-post. By keeping the end of the painter in his hand the canoeist whose canoe ran aground could jump out and feel sure that the canoe could not run away from him, and that he could not turn her broadside to the stream by hauling on the painter, as would have been the case had the painter been rove through the stem-post.

"I want to see that Sherbrooke postmaster!" exclaimed Joe, after running what was the seventh rapid, counting from the dam at Magog. "He said there were only one or two little rapids in this river. Why, there isn't anything but rapids in it!"

"There's something else just ahead of us worse than rapids," said Charley. "Look at that smoke."

Just a little distance below the fleet the river was completely hidden by a dense cloud of smoke that rested on the water and rose like a heavy fog-bank above the tops of the highest trees. It was caused by a fire in the woods—probably the very fire which the boys had started on the previous night. How far down the river the smoke extended, and whether any one could breathe while in it, were questions of great importance to the canoeists.

The fleet stopped just before reaching the smoke, and the boys backed water gently with their paddles while they discussed what they had better do. It was of no use to go ashore with the hope of finding how far the smoke extended, for it would have been as difficult to breathe on shore as on the water.

"There's one good thing about it," said Charley: "the smoke blows right across the river, so the chances are that it does not extend very far down stream."

"We can't hear the noise of any rapid," said Harry, "and that's another good thing. There can't be a rapid of any consequence within the next quarter of a mile."

"Then I'll tell you what I'll do, with the Commodore's permission," continued Charley. "There is no use in staying here all day, for that smoke may last for any length of time. I'll tie a wet handkerchief around my mouth and nose, and take the chances of paddling through the smoke. It isn't as thick close to the water as it looks to be, and I haven't the least doubt that I can run through it all right."

"But suppose you get choked with smoke, or get into a dangerous rapid?" suggested Tom.

"There isn't any rapid near us, or we would hear it, and I don't think the smoke will hurt me while I breathe through a wet handkerchief. At any rate, I'd rather try it than sit here and wait for the smoke to disappear."

It was decided, after farther discussion, that Charley should attempt to paddle through the smoke, if he really wished to do so; and that he should blow a whistle if he got through all right, and thought that the other boys could safely follow his example. Paddling a little way up stream, so as to have room to get up his fastest rate of speed before reaching the smoke, Charley started on his hazardous trip. He disappeared in the smoke with his canoe rushing along at a tremendous rate, and in a few seconds his comrades heard him calling to them to come on without fear.

They followed Charley's example in covering their mouths and noses with wet handkerchiefs, and in paddling at the top of their speed. They were agreeably surprised to find that the belt of smoke was only a few yards wide, and that almost before they had begun to find any difficulty in breathing they emerged into pure air and sunlight.

"It was a risky business for you, Charley," said Harry, "for the smoke might have covered the river for the next quarter of a mile."

"But then it didn't, you see," replied Charley. "How cheap we should have felt if we had waited till morning for the smoke to blow away, and then found that we could have run through it as easily as we have done!"

"Still, I say it was risky."

"Well, admitting that it was, what then? We can't go canoeing unless we are ready to take risks occasionally. If nobody is ever to take a risk, there ought not to be any canoes, or ships, or railroads."

"That Sherbrooke postmaster isn't afraid to take

risks," observed Joe. "If he keeps on telling canoeists that there are no rapids in this river, some of these days he'll have an accident with a large canoeist and a heavy paddle. We've run seven rapids already, and have another one ahead of us. If we ever get to Sherbrooke, I think it will be our duty to consider whether that postmaster ought to be allowed to live any longer."

Just before sunset the fleet reached Magog Lake, a placid sheet of water about four miles long, with three or four houses scattered along its eastern shore. At one of these houses eggs, milk, butter, bread, a chicken, and a raspberry pie were bought, and the boys went into camp near the lower end of the lake. After a magnificent supper they went to bed rather proud of their achievements during the last day and night.

The next day the canoeists started in the cool of the morning, and as soon as they left the lake found themselves at the head of their eighth rapid. All that day they paddled down the river, running rapids every little while, jumping overboard when their canoes ran aground and refused to float, and occasionally slipping on the smooth rocky bottom of the stream and sitting down violently in the water. Once they came to a dam, over which the canoes had to be lowered, and on the brink of which Joe slipped and slid with awful swiftness into the pool below, from which he escaped with no other injury than torn trousers and wet clothes.

"That postmaster said there were no dams in the Magog, didn't he?" asked Joe as he prepared to get into his canoe. "Well, I hope he hasn't any family."

"Why, what about his family?" demanded Tom.

"Nothing; only I'm going to try to get him to come down the Magog in a canoe, so he can see what a nice run it is. I suppose his body will be found some time, unless the bears get at him."

"That's all rubbish, Joe," said Charley. "We wouldn't have had half the fun we've had if there hadn't been any rapids in the river. We're none the worse for getting a little wet."

"We might have had less fun, but then I'd have had more trousers if it hadn't been for that dam. I like fun as well as anybody, but I can't land at Sherbrooke with these trousers."

"I see Sherbrooke now!" exclaimed Harry; "so you'd better change your clothes while you have a chance."

Sherbrooke was coming rapidly into sight as the fleet paddled down the stream, and in the course of half an hour the boys landed in the village, near a dam which converted the swift Magog into a lazy little pond. While his comrades drew the canoes out of the water and made them ready to be carted to the St. Francis, Harry went to engage a cart. He soon returned with a big wagon large enough to take two canoes at once; and it was not long before the fleet was resting in the shade on the bank of the St. Francis, and surrounded by a crowd of inquisitive men, boys, and girls.

It was difficult to convince the men that the canoes had actually come from Lake Memphremagog by the river, and the boys were made very proud of their success in running rapids which, the men declared, could only be run in skiffs during a freshet. Without an exception all the men agreed that there were rapids in the St. Francis which were really impassable, and that it would be foolish for the boys to think of descending that river. After making careful inquiries, and convincing themselves that the men were in earnest, the canoeists retired some distance from the crowd and held a council.

"The question is," said Harry, "shall we try the St. Francis after what we have heard? The youngest officer present will give his opinion first. What do you say, Joe?"

"I think I've had rapids and dams enough," replied Joe; "and I'd rather try some river where we can sail. I vote against the St. Francis."

"What do you say, Tom?"

"I'll do anything the rest of you like; but I think we'd better give the St. Francis up."

"Now, Charley, how do you vote?"

"For going down the St. Francis. I don't believe these men know much about the river, or anything about canoes. Let's stick to our original plan."

"There are two votes against the St. Francis, and one for it," said Harry. "I don't want to make a tie, so I'll vote with the majority. Boys, we won't go down the St. Francis, but we'll go to the hotel, stay there over Sunday, and decide where we will cruise next."

"All right," said Joe, going to his canoe, and taking a paddle blade in his hand.

"What in the world are you going to take that paddle to the hotel for?" asked Harry.

"I'm going to see the postmaster who said there were no rapids in the Magog or the St. Francis; that's all," replied Joe. "I've a painful duty to perform, and I'm going to perform it."

Chapter VII.

A COUNCIL was held at the hotel, and a dozen different water-routes were discussed. As the boys still wanted to carry out their original design of making a voyage to Quebec, they decided to take the canoes by rail to Rouse's Point, and from thence to descend the Richelieu River to the St. Lawrence. The railway journey would take nearly a whole day, but they thought it would be a rather pleasant change from the close confinement of canoeing. For it must be admitted that, delightful as they had found canoeing to be, the task of sitting for hours in the cockpit of a canoe with scarcely a possibility of materially changing one's position was tiresome, and the boys, after a night's sleep at the Sherbrooke hotel, felt decidedly stiff.

As it would have taken three days to send the canoes to Rouse's Point by freight, the canoeists were compelled to take them on the same train with themselves. They went to the express office on Monday morning and tried to make a bargain with the express company. The agent astonished them by the enormous price which he demanded, and Harry, who acted as spokesman for the expedition, told him that it was outrageous to ask such a price for carrying four light canoes.

The man turned to a book in which were contained the express company's rates of charges, and showed Harry that there was a fixed rate for row-boats and shells.

"But," said Harry, "a canoe is not a row-boat nor a shell. What justice is there in charging as much for a fourteen-foot canoe as for a forty-foot shell?"

"Well," said the agent, "I dunno as it would be fair. But, then, these canoes of yours are pretty near as big as row-boats."

"A canoe loaded as ours are don't weigh over one

hundred and ten pounds. How much does a row boat weigh?"

"Well, about two or three hundred pounds."

"Then, is it fair to charge as much for a canoe as for a row-boat, that weighs three times as much?"

The agent found it difficult to answer this argument, and after thinking the matter over he agreed to take the canoes at half the rate ordinarily charged for row-boats. The boys were pleased with their victory over him, but they still felt that to be compelled to pay four times as much for the canoes as they paid for their own railroad-tickets was an imposition.

At ten o'clock the train rolled into the Sherbrooke station. To the great disappointment of the boys, no express-car was attached to it, the only place for express packages being a small compartment twelve feet long at one end of the smoking-car. It was obvious that canoes fourteen feet long could not go into a space only twelve feet long, and it seemed as if it would be necessary to wait twelve hours for the night-train, to which a large express-car was always attached. But the conductor of the train was a man who could sympathize with boys, and who had ideas of his own. He uncoupled the engine, which was immediately in front of the smoking-car, and then had the canoes taken in through the door of the smoking-car and placed on the backs of the seats. Very little room was left for passengers who wanted to smoke; but as there were only four or five of these they made no complaint. The canoes, with blankets under them, to protect the backs of the seats, rode safely, and when, late in the afternoon, Rouse's Point, was reached, they were taken out of the car without a scratch.

There was just time enough before sunset to paddle a short distance below the fort, where a camping-ground was found that would have been very pleasant had there been fewer mosquitoes. They were the first Canadian mosquitoes that had made the acquaintance of the young canoeists, and they seemed to be delighted. They sung and buzzed in quiet excitement, and fairly drove the boys from their supper to the shelter of the canoes.

Harry had a long piece of mosquito-netting, which he threw over the top of his canoe-tent, and which fell over the openings on each side of the tent, thus protecting the occupant of the canoe from mosquitoes without depriving him of air. None of the other boys had taken the trouble to bring mosquito-netting with them, except Charley, who had a sort of mosquito-netting bag, which he drew over his head, and which prevented the mosquitoes from getting at his face and neck.

As for Joe and Tom, the mosquitoes fell upon them with great enthusiasm, and soon reduced them to a most miserable condition. Tom was compelled to cover his head with his India-rubber blanket, and was nearly suffocated. Joe managed to tie a handkerchief over his face in such a way as to allow himself air enough to breathe, and at the same time to keep off the mosquitoes. Instead of covering the rest of his body with his blanket, he deliberately exposed a bare arm and part of a bare leg, in hopes that he could thus satisfy the mosquitoes and induce them to be merciful. At the end of half an hour both Tom and Joe felt that they could endure the attacks of the insatiable insects no longer. They got up, and, stirring the embers of the fire, soon started a cheerful blaze. There were plenty of hemlock-trees close at hand, and the hemlock-boughs when thrown on the fire gave out a great deal of smoke. The two unfortunate boys sat in the lee of the fire and nearly choked themselves with smoke; but they could endure the smoke better than the mosquitoes, and so they were left alone by the latter. In the course of the next hour a breeze sprung up, which blew the mosquitoes away, and the sleepy and nearly stifled boys were permitted to go to bed and to sleep.

The wind died down before morning, and the mosquitoes returned. As soon as it was light the canoeists made haste to get breakfast and to paddle out into the stream. The mosquitoes let them depart without attempting to follow them; and the boys,

GETTING BREAKFAST UNDER DIFFICULTIES.

anchoring the canoes by making the ballast-bags fast to the painters, enjoyed an unmolested bath. As they were careful to anchor where the water was not quite four feet deep they had no difficulty in climbing into the canoes after the bath. Joe's mishap on Lake Memphremagog had taught them that getting into a canoe in deep water was easier in theory than in practice.

Later in the morning the usual southerly breeze, which is found almost every morning on the Richelieu, gave the canoeists the opportunity of making sail—an opportunity that was all the more welcome since the cruise down the Magog had been exclusively a paddling cruise. The breeze was just fresh enough to make it prudent for the canoes to carry their main-sails only, and to give the canoeists plenty of employment in watching the gusts that came through the openings in the woods that lined the western shore.

About twelve miles below Rouse's Point the fleet reached "Ile aux Noix," a beautiful island, in the middle of the stream, with a somewhat dilapidated fort at its northern end. The boys landed and examined the fort, and the ruined barracks which stood near it. The ditch surrounding the fort was half filled with the wooden palisades which had rotted and fallen into it, and large trees had sprung up on the grassy slope of the outer wall. The interior was, however, in good repair, and in one of the granite casemates lived an Irishman and his wife, who were the entire garrison. In former years the "Ile aux Noix" fort was one of the most important defences of the Canadian frontier, and even in its present forlorn condition it could be defended much longer than could the big American fort at Rouse's Point. The boys greatly enjoyed their visit to the island, and after lunch set sail, determined to make the most of the fair wind and to reach St. John before night.

The breeze held, and in less than three hours the steeples and the railway bridge of St. John came in view. The canoeists landed at the upper end of the town; and Harry and Charley, leaving the canoes in charge of the other boys, went in search of the Custom-house officer whose duty it was to inspect all vessels passing from the United States into Canada by way of the Richelieu River. Having found the officer, who was a very pleasant man, and who gave the fleet permission to proceed on its way without searching the canoes for smuggled goods, Harry and Charley walked on to examine the rapids, which begin just below the railway bridge. From St. John to Chambly, a distance of twelve miles, the river makes a rapid descent, and is entirely unnavigable for anything except canoes. A canal around the rapids enables canal boats and small vessels to reach the river at Chambly, where it again becomes navigable; but the boys did not like the idea of paddling through the canal, and greatly preferred to run the rapids.

The first rapid was a short but rough one. Still, it was no worse than the first of the Magog rapids, and Harry and Charley made up their minds that it could be safely run. The men of whom they made inquiries as to the rapids farther down said that they were impassable, and that the canoes had better pass directly into the canal, without attempting to run even the first rapid. Harry was inclined to think that this advice was good, but Charley pointed out that it would be possible to drag the canoes up the bank of the river and launch them in the canal at any point between St. John and Chambly, and that it would be time enough to abandon the river when it should really prove to be impassable.

Returning to the canoes, the Commodore gave the order to prepare to run the rapids. In a short time the fleet, with the *Sunshine* in advance, passed under the bridge; and narrowly escaping shipwreck on the remains of the wooden piles that once supported a bridge that had been destroyed by fire, entered the rapid. There was quite a crowd gathered to watch the canoes as they passed, but those people who wanted the excitement of seeing the canoes wrecked were disappointed. Not a drop of water found its way into the cockpit of a single canoe; and though there was an ugly rock near the end of the rapid, against which each canoeist fully expected to be driven as he approached it, the run was made without the slightest accident.

Drifting down with the current a mile or two below the town, the boys landed and encamped for the night. While waiting at St. John, Joe and Tom had provided themselves with mosquito-netting, but they had little use for it, for only a few mosquitoes made the discovery that four healthy and attractive boys were within reach. The night was cool and quiet, and the canoeists, tired with their long day's work, slept until late in the morning.

Everything was prepared the next day for running the rapids which the men at St. John had declared to be impassable. The spars and all the stores were lashed fast; the sand-bags were placed in the after-compartments; the painters were rove through the stern-posts, and the life-belts were placed where they could be buckled on at an instant's notice. After making all these preparations it was rather disappointing to find no rapids whatever between St.

John and Chambly, or rather the Chambly railway bridge.

"It just proves what I said yesterday," remarked Charley, turning round in his canoe to speak to his comrades, who were a boat's length behind him. "People who live on the banks of a river never know anything about it. Now, I don't believe there is a rapid in the whole Richelieu River, except at St. John. Halloo! keep back, boys—"

While he was speaking Charley and his canoe disappeared as suddenly as if the earth, or rather the water, had opened and swallowed them. The other boys in great alarm backed water, and then paddling ashore as fast as possible, sprung out of their canoes and ran along the shore, to discover what had become of Charley. They found him at the foot of a water-fall of about four feet in height over which he had been carried. The fall was formed by a long ledge of rock running completely across the river; and had the boys been more careful, and had the wind been blowing in any other direction than directly down the river, they would have heard the sound of the falling water in time to be warned of the danger into which Charley had carelessly run.

His canoe had sustained little damage, for it had luckily fallen where the water was deep enough to keep it from striking the rocky bottom. Charley had been thrown out as the canoe went over the fall, but had merely bruised himself a little. He towed his canoe ashore, and in answer to a mischievous question from Joe admitted that perhaps the men who had said that the Chambly rapids were impassable were right.

Below the fall and as far as the eye could reach stretched a fierce and shallow rapid. The water boiled over and among the rocks with which it was strewn, and there could not be any doubt that the rapid was one which could not be successfully run, unless, perhaps, by some one perfectly familiar with the channel. It was agreed that the canoes must be carried up to the canal, and after two hours of hard work the fleet was launched a short distance above one of the canal locks.

The lock-man did not seem disposed to let the canoes pass through the lock, but finally accepted fifty cents, and, grumbling to himself in his Canadian French, proceeded to lock the canoes through. He paid no attention to the request that he would open the sluices gradually, but opened them all at once and to their fullest extent. The result was that the water in the lock fell with great rapidity; the canoes were swung against one another and against the side of the lock, and Charley's canoe, catching against a bolt in one of the upper gates, was capsized and sunk to the bottom, leaving her captain clinging to the stern of the *Sunshine*.

Chapter VIII.

THERE is no place more unfit for a sudden and unexpected bath than the lock of a canal. The sides and the gates are perpendicular and smooth, and present nothing to which a person in the water can cling. Charley had no difficulty in supporting himself by throwing one arm over the stern of Harry's canoe, but had he been alone in the lock he would have been in a very unpleasant position.

As soon as the gates were opened the boys paddled out of the lock, and went ashore to devise a plan for raising the sunken canoe. Of course it was necessary that some one should dive and bring up the painter, so that the canoe could be dragged out of the lock; but, as canal boats were constantly passing, it was a full hour before any attempt at diving could be made. There were half a dozen small French boys playing near the lock, and Charley, who was by no means anxious to do any unnecessary diving, hired them to get the canoe ashore, which they managed to do easily. It was then found that nearly everything except the spars had floated out of her, and the rest of the morning was spent in searching for the missing articles in the muddy bottom of the canal. Most of them were recovered, but Charley's spare clothes, which were in an India-rubber bag, could not be found.

This was the second time that the unfortunate *Midnight* had foundered, and Charley was thoroughly convinced of the necessity of providing some means of keeping her afloat in case of capsizing. It was impossible for him to put water-tight compartments in her, such as the *Sunshine* and the *Dawn* possessed, but he resolved to buy a dozen beef-bladders at the next town, and after blowing them up to pack them in the bow and stern of his canoe. Tom, whose "Rice Lake" canoe was also without water-tight compartments, agreed to adopt Charley's plan, and thus avoid running the risk of an accident that might result in the loss of the canoe and cargo.

When the fleet finally got under way again there was a nice breeze from the south, which sent the canoes along at the rate of four or five miles an hour. Chambly, the northern end of the canal, was reached before four o'clock, the boys having lunched on bread-and-water while in the canoes in order not to lose time by going ashore. They passed safely through the three great locks at Chambly; and entering the little lake formed by the expansion of the river, and known as Chambly Basin, they skirted its northern shore until they reached the ruins of Chambly Castle.

More than one hundred and fifty years ago the Frenchmen built the great square fort, with round towers at each angle, which is now called Chambly Castle. At that time the only direct way of communication between the settlements on the St. Lawrence and those in the valleys of the Hudson and the Mohawk was up the Richelieu River, Lake Champlain, and Lake George. It was this route that Burgoyne followed when he began the campaign that ended so disastrously for him at Saratoga, and it was at Chambly Castle that he formally took command of his army. The castle was placed just at the foot of the rapids, on a broad, level space, where Indians used to assemble in large numbers to trade with the French. Its high stone walls, while they could easily have been knocked to pieces by cannon, were a complete protection against the arrows and rifles of the savages, and could have withstood a long siege by any English force not provided with artillery. In the old days when the castle was garrisoned by gay young French officers, and parties of beautiful ladies came up from Montreal to attend the officers' balls, and the gray old walls echoed to music, and brilliant lights flashed through the windows, the Indians encamped outside the gates must have thought it the most magnificent and brilliant place in the whole world. Now there is nothing left of it but the four walls and the crumbling towers. The iron bolts on which the great castle gate once swung are still embedded in the stone, but nothing else remains inside the castle except grassy mounds and the wild vines that climb wherever they can find an angle or a stone to cling to.

The canoeists made their camp where the Indians had so often camped before them, and after supper they rambled through the castle and climbed to the top of one of the towers. They had never heard of its existence, and were as surprised as they were delighted to find so romantic a ruin.

"I haven't the least doubt that the place is full of ghosts," said Charley as the boys were getting into the canoes for the night.

"Do you really believe in ghosts?" asked Tom, in his matter-of-fact way.

"Why," replied Charley, "when you think of what must have happened inside of that old castle and outside of it when the Indians tortured their prisoners, there can't help but be ghosts here."

"I don't care, provided there are no mosquitoes," said Joe. "Ghosts don't bite, and don't sing in a fellow's ears."

Any one who has camped near a rapid knows how strangely the running water sounds in the stillness of the night. Joe, who, although there were no mosquitoes to trouble him, could not fall asleep, was sure that he heard men's voices talking in a low tone, and two or three times raised himself up in his canoe to see if there were any persons in sight. He became convinced after a while that the sounds which disturbed him were made by the water, but, nevertheless, they had made him rather nervous. Though he had professed not to be afraid of ghosts, he did not like to think about them, but he could not keep them out of his mind. Once, when he looked out of his canoe toward the castle, he was startled to find it brilliantly lighted up. The light was streaming from the casemates, loop-holes, and windows, and it was some moments before he comprehended that it was nothing more ghostly than moonlight.

Toward midnight Joe fell asleep, but he slept uneasily. He woke up suddenly to find a dark object with two fiery eyes seated on the deck of his canoe and apparently watching him. He sprung up, with a cry of terror, which awakened his comrades. The strange object rushed away from the canoe, and, stopping near the gate of the castle, seemed to be waiting to see what the boys would do.

By this time Joe had recovered his senses, and knew that his strange visitor was a wild animal. The boys took their pistols. Tom, who was the best shot, fired at the animal. He did not hit it, but as Tom advanced slowly toward it the creature went into the castle.

"It's a wild-cat," cried Charley. "I saw it as it crossed that patch of moonlight. Come on, boys, and we'll have a hunt."

With their pistols ready for instant service, the canoeists rushed into the castle. The wild-cat was seated on a pile of stones in what was once the courtyard, and did not show any signs of fear. Three or four pistol-shots, however, induced it to spring down from its perch and run across the court-yard. The boys followed it eagerly, plunging into a thick growth of tall weeds, and shouting at the top of their lungs. Suddenly the animal vanished; and though Tom fancied that he saw it crouching in the shadow of the wall and fired at it, as he supposed, he soon found that he was firing at a piece of old stove-pipe that had probably been brought to the place by a picnic party.

Giving up the hunt with reluctance, the canoeists returned to their canoes; at least, three of them did, but Joe was not with them. They called to him, but received no answer, and becoming anxious about him, went back to the castle and shouted his name loudly, but without success.

"It's very strange," exclaimed Charley. "He was close behind me when we chased the wild-cat into those weeds."

"Has anybody seen him since?" asked Harry.

Nobody had seen him.

HUNTING FOR A WILD-CAT IN CHAMBLY CASTLE.

"Then," said Harry, "the wild-cat has carried him off, or killed him."

"Nonsense!" exclaimed Charley; "a wild-cat isn't a tiger, and couldn't carry off a small baby. Joe must be trying to play a trick on us."

"Let's go back and pay no attention to him," suggested Tom. "I don't like such tricks."

"There's no trick about it," said Harry. "Joe isn't that kind of fellow. Something has happened to him, and we've got to look for him till we find him."

"Harry's right," said Charley. "Go and get the lantern out of my canoe, won't you, Tom? I've got matches in my pocket."

When the lantern was lit a careful search was made all over the court-yard. Harry was greatly frightened, for he was afraid that Joe might have been accidentally shot while the boys were shooting at the wild-cat, and he remembered that in his excitement he had fired his pistol in a very reckless way. It was horrible to think that he might have shot poor Joe; worse, even, than thinking that the wildcat might have seized him.

The court-yard had been thoroughly searched without finding the least trace of Joe, and the boys were becoming more and more alarmed, when Charley, whose ears were particularly sharp, cried, "Hush! I hear something." They all listened intently, and heard a voice faintly calling "Help!" They knew at once that it was Joe's voice, but they could not imagine where he was. They shouted in reply to him, and Charley, seizing the lantern, carefully pushed aside the tall weeds and presently found himself at the mouth of a well.

"Are you there, Joe?" he cried, lying down on the ground, with his head over the mouth of the well.

"I believe I am," replied Joe. "I'm ready to come out, though, if you fellows will help me."

The boys gave a great shout of triumph.

"Are you hurt?" asked Charley, eagerly.

"I don't think I am; but I think somebody will be if I have to stay here much longer."

It was evident that Joe was not seriously hurt, although he had fallen into the well while rushing recklessly after the wild-cat. Tom and Harry ran to the canoes and returned with all four of the canoe-painters. Tying one of them to the lantern, Charley lowered it down, and was able to get a glimpse of Joe. The well was about twenty feet deep, and perfectly dry, and Joe was standing, with his hands in his pockets, leaning against the side of the well, and apparently entirely unhurt, in spite of his fall.

Chapter IX.

IT was an easy matter to help Joe out of the old well. He had fallen into it while running after the wild-cat, but a heap of decayed leaves at the bottom broke the fall and saved him from any serious injury. Nevertheless, he must have been a little stunned at first, for he made no outcry for some time, and it was his first call for help that was heard by Charley.

The boys returned to their canoes, and, as it was not yet midnight, prepared to resume the sleep from which they had been so unceremoniously awakened. They had little fear that the wild-cat would pay them another visit, for it had undoubtedly been badly frightened. Still, it was not pleasant to think that there was a wild beast within a few rods of them, and the thought kept the canoeists awake for a long time.

The wild-cat did not pay them a second visit, and when they awoke the next morning they were half inclined to think that their night's adventure had been only a dream. There, however, were the marks made by its claws on the varnished deck of Joe's canoe, and Joe's clothing was torn and stained by his fall. With the daylight they became very courageous, and decided that they had never been in the least afraid of the animal. The so-called wild-cat of Canada, which is really a lynx, is, however, a fierce and vicious animal, and is sometimes more than a match for an unarmed man.

There was a strong west wind blowing when the fleet started, and Chambly Basin was covered with white-caps. As the canoes were sailing in the trough of the sea they took in considerable water while skirting the east shore of the Basin, but once in the narrow river they found the water perfectly smooth. This day the fleet made better progress than on any previous day. Nothing could be more delightful than the scenery, and the quaint little French towns along the river, every one of which was named after some saint, were very interesting. The boys landed at one of them and got their dinner at a little tavern where no one spoke English, and where Charley, who had studied French at Annapolis, won the admiration of his comrades by the success with which he ordered the dinner.

With the exception of the hour spent at dinner, the canoeists sailed, from six o'clock in the morning until seven at night, at the rate of nearly six miles an hour. The clocks of Sorel, the town at the mouth of the Richelieu, were striking six as the canoes glided into the broad St. Lawrence and steered for a group of islands distant about a mile from the south shore. It was while crossing the St. Lawrence that they first made the acquaintance of screw-steamers, and learned how dangerous they are to the careless canoeist. A big steamship, on her way to Montreal, came up the river so noiselessly that the boys did

not notice her until they heard her hoarse whistle warning them to keep out of her way. A paddle-wheel steamer can be heard while she is a long way off, but screw-steamers glide along so stealthily that the English canoeists, who constantly meet them on the Mersey, the Clyde, and the lower Thames, have nicknamed them "sudden death."

Cramped and tired were the canoeists when they reached the nearest island and went ashore to prepare a camp, but they were proud of having sailed sixty miles in one day. As they sat around the fire after supper Harry said, "Boys, we've had experience enough by this time to test our different rigs. Let's talk about them a little."

"All right," said Joe. "I want it understood, however, that my lateen is by all odds the best rig in the fleet."

"Charley," remarked Tom, "you said the other day that you liked Joe's rig better than any other. Do you think so still?"

"Of course I do," answered Charley. "Joe's sails

set flatter than any lug-sail; he can set them and take them in quicker than we can handle ours, and as they are triangular he has the most of his canvas at the foot of the sail instead of at the head. But they're going to spill him before the cruise is over, or I'm mistaken."

"In what way?" asked Joe.

"You are going to get yourself into a scrape some day by trying to take in your sail when you are running before a stiff breeze. If you try to get the sail down without coming up into the wind it will get overboard, and either you will lose it or it will capsize you; you tried it yesterday when a squall came up, and you very nearly came to grief."

"But you can say the same about any other rig," exclaimed Joe.

"Of course you can't very well get any sail down while the wind is in it; but Tom can take in his sharpie-sail without much danger even when he's running directly before the wind, and Harry and I can let go our halyards and get our lugs down after a fashion, if it is necessary. Still, your lateen is the best cruising rig I've ever seen, though for racing Harry's big, square-headed balance-lug is better."

"You may say what you will," said Tom, "but give me my sharpie-sails. They set as flat as a board, and I can handle them easily enough to suit me."

"The trouble with your rig," said Charley, "is that you have a mast nearly fifteen feet high. Now, when Joe takes in his main-sail he has only two feet of mast left standing."

"How do you like your own rig?" asked Harry.

"Oh, it is good enough. I'm not sure that it isn't better than either yours or Tom's; but it certainly isn't as handy as Joe's lateen."

"Now that you've settled that I've the best rig," said Joe, "you'd better admit that I've the best canoe, and then turn in for the night. After the work we've done to-day, and the fun we had last night, I'm sleepy."

"Do you call sitting still in a canoe hard work?" inquired Tom.

"Is falling down a well your idea of fun?" asked Harry.

"It's too soon," said Charley, "to decide who has the best canoe. We'll find that out by the time the cruise is over."

The island where the boys camped during their first night on the St. Lawrence was situated at the head of Lake St. Peter. This lake is simply an expansion of the St. Lawrence, and though it is thirty miles long and about ten miles wide at its widest part, it is so shallow that steamboats can only pass through it by following an artificial channel dredged out by the government at a vast expense. Its shores are lined with a thick growth of reeds, which extend in many places fully a mile into the lake, and are absolutely impassable, except where streams flowing into the lake have kept channels open through the reeds.

On leaving the island in the morning the canoeists paddled down the lake, for there was not a breath of wind. The sun was intensely hot, and the heat reflected from the surface of the water and the varnished decks of the canoes assisted in making the boys feel as if they were roasting before a fire. Toward noon the heat became really intolerable, and the Commodore gave the order to paddle over to the north shore in search of shade.

It was disappointing to find instead of a shady shore an impenetrable barrier of reeds. After resting a little while in the canoes, the boys started to skirt the reeds, in hope of finding an opening; and the sun, apparently taking pity on them, went under a cloud, so that they paddled a mile or two in comparative comfort.

The friendly cloud was followed before long by a mass of thick black clouds coming up from the south. Soon the thunder was heard in the distance, and it dawned upon the tired boys that they were about to have a thunder-storm, without any opportunity of obtaining shelter.

They paddled steadily on, looking in vain for a path through the reeds, and making up their minds to a good wetting. They found, however, that the rain did not come alone. With it came a fierce gust of wind, which quickly raised white-caps on the lake. Instead of dying out as soon as the rain fell the wind blew harder and harder, and in the course of half an hour there was a heavy sea running.

The wind and sea coming from the south, while the canoes were steering east, placed the boys in a very dangerous position. The seas struck the canoes on the side and broke over them, and in spite of the aprons, which to some extent protected the cockpits of all except the *Twilight*, the water found its way below. It was soon no longer possible to continue in the trough of the sea, and the canoes were compelled to turn their bows to the wind and sea—the boys paddling just sufficiently to keep themselves from drifting back into the reeds.

The *Sunshine* and the *Midnight* behaved admirably, taking very little water over their decks. The *Twilight* "slapped" heavily, and threw showers of spray over herself, while the *Dawn* showed a tendency to dive bodily into the seas, and several times the whole of her forward of the cockpit was under the water.

"What had we better do?" asked Harry, who, although Commodore, had the good-sense always to consult Charley in matters of seamanship.

"It's going to blow hard, and we can't sit here and paddle against it all day without getting exhausted."

"But how are we going to help ourselves?" continued Harry.

"Your canoe and mine," replied Charley, "can live out the gale well enough under sail. If we set our main-sails close-reefed, and keep the canoes close to the wind, we shall be all right. It's the two other canoes that I'm troubled about."

"My canoe suits me well enough," said Joe, "so long as she keeps on the top of the water, but she seems to have made up her mind to dive under it."

"Mine would be all right if I could stop paddling long enough to bail her out, but I can't," remarked Tom. "She's nearly half full of water now."

"We can't leave the other fellows," said Harry, "so what's the use of our talking about getting sail on our canoes?"

"It's just possible that Tom's canoe would live under sail," resumed Charley; "but it's certain that Joe's won't. What do you think about those reeds, Tom—can you get your canoe into them?"

"Of course I can, and that's what we'd better all do," exclaimed Tom. "The reeds will break the force of the seas, and we can stay among them till the wind goes down."

"Suppose you try it," suggested Charley, "and let us see how far you can get into the reeds? I think they're going to help us out of a very bad scrape."

Tom did not dare to turn his canoe around, so he backed water and went at the reeds stern-first. They parted readily, and his canoe penetrated without much difficulty some half-dozen yards into the reeds where the water was almost quiet. Unfortunately, he shipped one heavy sea just as he entered the reeds, which filled his canoe so full that another such sea would certainly have sunk her, had she not been provided with the bladders bought at Chambly.

Joe followed Tom's example, but the *Dawn* perversely stuck in the reeds just as she was entering them, and sea after sea broke over her before Joe could drive her far enough into the reeds to be protected by them.

Joe and Tom were now perfectly safe, though miserably wet; but, as the rain had ceased, there was nothing to prevent them from getting dry clothes out of their water-proof bags, and putting them on as soon as they could bail the water out of their canoes. Harry and Charley, seeing their comrades in safety, made haste to get up sail and to stand out into the lake—partly because they did not want to run the risk of being swamped when entering the reeds, and partly because they wanted the excitement of sailing in a gale of wind.

When the masts were stepped, the sails hoisted, and the sheets trimmed, the two canoes, sailing close to the wind, began to creep away from the reeds.

They behaved wonderfully well. The boys had to watch them closely, and to lean out to windward from time to time to hold them right side up. The rudders were occasionally thrown out of the water, but the boys took the precaution to steer with their paddles. The excitement of sailing was so great, that Charley and Harry forgot all about the time, and sailed on for hours. Suddenly they discovered that it was three o'clock, that they had had no lunch, and that the two canoeists who had sought refuge in the reeds had absolutely nothing to eat with them. Filled with pity, they resolved to return to them without a moment's delay. It was then that it occurred to them that in order to sail back they must turn their canoes around, bringing them while so doing in the trough of the sea. Could they possibly do this without being swamped? The question was a serious one, for they were fully four miles from the shore, and the wind and sea were as high as ever.

Chapter X.

CHARLEY and Harry took in their sails, keeping the canoes head to sea with an occasional stroke of the paddle. When all was made snug, and the moment for turning the canoes had arrived, they realized that they were about to attempt the most hazardous feat of the whole cruise.

"Can we do it?" asked Harry, doubtfully.

"We've got to do it," replied Charley.

"Why can't we unship our rudders and back water till we get to the reeds?"

"It might be possible, but the chances are that we would be swamped. The seas would overtake us, and we couldn't keep out of the way of them. No, we've got to turn around and sail back in the regular way."

"You know best, of course," said Harry; "but what's the use of taking in our sails before we turn around? We'll have trouble in setting them again with the wind astern."

"We can turn the canoes quicker without sails than we could with the sails set, and every second that we can gain is worth something. Besides, if we are capsized it will be an advantage to have the sails furled. But we're wasting time. Let your canoe get right astern of mine, so that mine will keep a little of the sea off of you; then watch for two or three big seas and turn your canoe when they have passed."

Harry followed his friend's instructions, and succeeded in turning his canoe without accident. Then Charley, getting into the lee of the *Sunshine*, did his best to imitate Harry's successful feat. He managed to turn the canoe, but while in the act a heavy sea rolled into the cockpit and filled the *Midnight* absolutely full. The beef-bladders, however, kept the canoe afloat, but she lay like a log on the water, and every successive wave swept over her.

Charley did not lose his presence of mind. He shouted to Harry to run up his sail and keep his canoe out of the way of the seas, and then he busied himself shaking out the reef of his main-sail, so that he could set the whole sail. The moment the canoe felt the strain of her canvas she began to rush through the water in spite of her great weight, and no more seas came aboard her. Steering with one hand, Charley bailed with his hat with such energy that he soon freed the canoe of water. Meanwhile he rapidly overtook Harry, and reached the reeds, while the *Sunshine* was a quarter of a mile behind him.

Tom and Joe were found sitting in their canoes and suffering the pangs of hunger. Charley put on dry clothes, while Harry prepared a lunch of dried beef and crackers, after which the canoeists resigned themselves as cheerfully as they could to spending the rest of the afternoon and the night in the reeds. It was not a pleasant place, but the wind kept the mosquitoes away, and the boys managed to fall asleep soon after sunset. The wind died out during the night, and the boys found, the next morning, that only a few rods below the place where they had spent the night there was an open channel by which they could easily have reached the shore. This was rather aggravating, and it increased the disgust with which they remembered Lake St. Peter and its reed-lined shores.

The voyage down the St. Lawrence seemed monotonous after the excitement of running the Magog rapids, and the various adventures of the sail down the Richelieu. The St. Lawrence has very little shade along its banks, for, owing to the direction in which it runs, the sun shines on the water all day long. The weather was exceedingly hot while the boys were on the river, and on the third day after leaving Lake St. Peter they suffered so greatly that they were afraid to stay on the water lest they should be sunstruck. Going ashore on the low sandy bank, they were unable to find a single tree or even a hillock large enough to afford any shade. They thought of drawing the canoes ashore and sitting in the

A Quicksand.

shade of them, but there was not a breath of air stirring, and the very ground was so hot that it almost scorched their feet. Half a mile away on a meadow they saw a tree, but it was far too hot to think of walking that distance. They decided at last to get into their canoes and to paddle a few rods farther to a place where a small stream joined the river, and where they hoped to find the water somewhat cooler for bathing.

On reaching the mouth of the little stream the bows of the canoes were run ashore, so that they would not float away, and the boys, hastily undressing, sprung into the water. They had a delightful bath, and it was not until they began to feel chilly that they thought of coming out and dressing. Tom was the first to go ashore, and as he was wading out of the water he suddenly felt himself sinking in the sand. Harry and Joe attempted to land a few yards from the place where Tom was trying to drag his feet out of the clinging sand, and they too found themselves in the same difficulty. Harry at once perceived what was the matter, and, making frantic efforts to get to the shore, cried out to his comrades that they were caught in a quicksand.

The struggles made by the three boys were all in vain. When they tried to lift one foot out of the sand the other foot would sink still deeper. It was impossible for them to throw themselves at full length on the quicksand, for there were nearly two feet of water over it, and they were not close enough together to give one another any assistance. By the time Charley fully understood the peril they were in, Tom had sunk above his knees in the sand, and Joe and Harry, finding that they could not extricate themselves, were waiting, with white faces and trembling lips, for Charley to come to their help.

Charley knew perfectly well that if he ventured too near the other boys he would himself be caught in the quicksand, and there would be no hope that any of them could escape. Keeping his presence of mind, he swum to the stern of one of the canoes, set it afloat, and pushed it toward Tom so that the latter could get hold of its bow. He then brought two other canoes to the help of Joe and Harry, and when each of the three unfortunate canoeists was thus furnished with something to cling to he climbed into his own canoe.

"What are we to do now?" asked Harry.

"Just hold on to your canoes till I can tow them out into the stream. You can't sink while you hang on to them."

"Won't the canoes sink with us?" asked Tom.

"Not a bit of it. You wouldn't sink yourselves if you could lie down flat on the quicksand. I was caught in a quicksand once, and that's the way I saved myself."

"I hope it's all right," exclaimed Joe; "but it seems to me that you'll have to get a derrick to hoist me out. But I'm not complaining. I can hang on to my canoe all day, only I don't want to be drowned and buried both at the same time."

Charley, meanwhile, was busily making his canoe fast to Tom's canoe with his painter. When this was done he paddled away from the shore with all his might, while Tom tried to lift himself out of the quicksand by throwing the weight of his body on the canoe. Slowly Tom and his canoe yielded to the vigorous strokes of Charley's paddle and were towed out into deep water. By the same means Joe and Harry were rescued, and then the entire fleet—Charley paddling, and the others swimming and pushing their canoes—floated a short distance down stream, and finally landed where the sand was firm and hard.

"What should we have done if you'd got into the quicksand, as we did?" said Harry to Charley, as they were dressing.

"By this time we should all have disappeared," replied Charley.

"I shall never go ashore again while we're on this river without making sure that I'm not walking into a quicksand," continued Harry. "It was awful to find myself sinking deeper and deeper, and to know that I couldn't help myself."

"Very likely there isn't another quicksand the

whole length of the St. Lawrence," said Charley. "However, it's well enough to be careful where we land. I've noticed that where a little stream joins a big one the bottom is likely to be soft; but after all a regular dangerous quicksand isn't often met. I never saw but one before."

"Tell us about it," suggested Joe.

"No; we've talked enough about quicksands, and the subject isn't a cheerful one. Do you see that pile of boards? Let's make a board shanty, and go to sleep in it after we've had some lunch. It will be too hot to paddle before the end of the afternoon."

A shanty was easily made by leaning a dozen planks against the top of the pile of boards, and after a comfortable lunch the boys took a long nap. When they awoke they were disgusted to find that their canoes were high and dry two rods from the edge of the water. They had reached a part of the river where the tide was felt, and without knowing it they had gone ashore at high tide. They had to carry the canoes, with all their contents, down to the water, and as the receding tide had left a muddy and slippery surface to walk over the task was not a pleasant one. They congratulated themselves that they had not gone ashore at low tide, in which case the rising of the water during the night would have carried away the canoes.

Sailing down the river with a gentle breeze, and with the help of the ebbing tide, the canoeists came to the mouth of a small river which entered the St. Lawrence from the north. They knew by means of the map that the small river was the Jacques Cartier. It was a swift, shallow, and noisy stream, flowing between high, precipitous banks, and spanned by a lofty and picturesque bridge. Taking in their sails, the boys entered the Jacques Cartier, picking their way carefully among the rocks, and making headway very slowly against the rapid current. They stopped under the bridge, just above which there was an impassable rapid, and went ashore for lunch.

Near by there was a saw-mill, and from one of the workmen who came to look at the canoes the boys heard wonderful reports of the fish to be caught in the stream. It was full of salmon—so the man said—and about nine miles from its mouth there was a pool where the trout actually clamored to be caught. The enthusiasm of the canoeists was kindled; and they resolved to make a camp on the bank of the stream, and to spend a few days in fishing.

After having thus excited his young hearers the workman cruelly told them that the right to fish for salmon was owned by a man living in Montreal, and that any one catching a salmon without permission would be heavily fined. The trout, however, belonged to nobody, and the boys, though greatly disappointed about the salmon, would not give up their plan of trout-fishing. They hired two carts from a farmer living a short distance from the river, and, placing their canoes on the carts, walked beside them over a wretchedly rough road until they reached a place deep in the woods, where a little stream, icy cold, joined the Jacques Cartier. Just before entering the latter the little stream formed a quiet pool, in which the trout could be seen jumping. The point of land between the trout-stream and the river was covered with a carpet of soft grass, and on this the canoes were placed and made ready to be slept in.

The workman at the mouth of the Jacques Cartier had not exaggerated the number of trout in the pool. It was alive with fish. The boys were charmed with the beauty of their camping-ground and the luxury of their table. It was rather tiresome to walk two miles every day to the nearest farm-house for milk, but with the milk rice griddle-cakes were made, and upon these and fresh-killed trout the canoeists feasted for three delightful days.

They had one real adventure while on the Jacques Cartier. One day, when they returned to their camp from an exploration of the upper part of the trout-stream, they found a bear feasting upon the remains of their breakfast and their bottle of maple-sirup, which he had upset and broken. The animal was full-grown, and looked like a very ugly customer, but no sooner did he see the boys than he started on

"THEY FOUND A BEAR FEASTING UPON THE REMAINS OF THEIR BREAKFAST."

a rapid run for the woods. By the time the boys had found their pistols and were ready to follow him the bear had disappeared, and though they hunted for him all the rest of the day they could not find him. Had the bear taken it into his head to hunt the boys he would probably have been much more successful, for their pistol-bullets would have had little effect upon him, except to sharpen his appetite for tender and wholesome boys'-meat.

Chapter XI.

IT sometimes blows very hard on the St. Lawrence. It blew especially hard the morning the young canoeists returned to the banks of the great river from their excursion up the Jacques Cartier. As far as they could see the St. Lawrence was covered with white-caps. The wind blew directly up the river, and a heavy sea was breaking on the little island which lay opposite the mouth of the Jacques Cartier. Paddling against such a wind and sea would have been nearly impossible, and the boys resolved to wait until the wind should go down.

The day was a long one, for there was nothing to do but to watch the men at work in the saw-mill, and to look out on the river to see if the wind and sea had gone down. It continued to blow hard all day and all night, and when Harry awoke his comrades at five o'clock the next morning it was blowing as hard as ever.

Nobody wanted to spend another day at the sawmill. Although the wind was blowing up the river the tide was ebbing, and would help the canoes to make some little progress, in spite of the wind and sea. So after a hurried breakfast the fleet got under way at six o'clock and gallantly breasted the waves.

The boys found that paddling against so strong a head-wind was harder than they had imagined that it could be. It was almost impossible to force the upper blade of the paddle through the air when trying to make a stroke, and it was only by turning the two paddle-blades at right angles to one another, so that the upper blade would present its edge to the wind, that this could be done. The seas were so large that the two canoes which were leading would often be entirely invisible to the other canoes, though they were but a few yards apart. The *Twilight,* as was her habit when driven against head-seas, threw spray all over herself, and the *Dawn* exhibited her old vice of trying to dive through the seas. The other canoes were dry enough, but they presented more resistance to the wind, and hence were harder to paddle.

Little was said during the first half-hour, for everybody was working too hard at the paddle to have any breath to spare for talking; but finally Harry, who was in the advance with Charley, slackened his stroke, and, hailing Joe and Tom, asked them how they were getting along.

"Wet as usual," replied Joe. "The water is pretty near up to my waist in the canoe, and two waves out of three wash right over her. But I don't care; I'll paddle as long as anybody else will."

"My canoe will float, unless the bladders burst," said Tom, "but I'll have to stop and bail out before long, or she'll be so heavy that I can't stir her."

"Never mind," cried Joe. "Look at the splendid time we're making. We've come nearly a quarter of a mile, and that means that we're paddling at the rate of half a mile an hour. At this rate we'll get somewhere in the course of the summer."

"There isn't any use in tiring ourselves out for nothing," exclaimed Harry. "Boys! we'll make that sand-spit right ahead of us, and wait there till the wind goes down."

"All right," said Joe. "Only it's a pity to go ashore when the tide is helping us along so beautifully. That is, the Commodore said it would help us, and of course he is right."

"No reflections on the Commodore will be allowed," cried Harry. "Bail out your canoes, you two fellows, and Charley and I will wait for you."

Joe was very anxious to go ashore and rest, for he was nearly tired out; but he was not willing to let Harry know that he was tired. The two boys had been disputing while on the Jacques Cartier as to their respective strength, and Harry had boasted that he could endure twice as much fatigue as Joe. This was true enough, for Harry was older and much more muscular, but Joe was determined to paddle as long as he could swing his arms rather than to admit that he was the weaker.

The sandy spit where Harry proposed to rest was half a mile farther on, but before it was reached poor Joe managed to sprain the muscles of his left wrist. He was compelled to stop paddling except just hard enough to keep the *Dawn's* head to the sea, and to call out to the Commodore that he must be allowed to go ashore at once.

Now, the north shore of the river, near which the canoes were paddling, was a rocky precipice, rising perpendicularly directly from the water, and at least two hundred feet high. To land on such a shore was, of course, impossible, and the sandy spit toward which the fleet was paddling was the only possible landing-place within sight, unless the canoes were to turn round and run back to the Jacques Cartier.

In this state of things Harry, after consulting with Charley and Tom, resolved to tow the *Dawn*. Her painter was made fast to the stern-post of the *Sunshine*, and Harry, bracing his feet and setting his teeth tight together, began the task of forcing two heavy canoes through the rough water. He found that he could make progress slowly, but Joe could not steer the *Dawn* except by paddling, and as he was able to do very little of that she kept yawing about in a most unpleasant way, which greatly added to Harry's labor.

Suddenly, Joe had a happy thought: he set his "dandy" and hauled the sheet taut, so that the boom was parallel with the keel. The effect of this was that whenever the canoe's head fell off the sail filled and brought her up again. Joe was relieved of the task of steering, and Harry was able to tow the *Dawn* much more easily than before.

The other canoeists followed Joe's example, and, setting their "dandies," greatly lessened their labor. The canoes kept their heads to the wind of their own accord, and everybody wondered why so obvious a method of fighting a head-wind had not sooner been thought of.

It was eight o'clock when the sandy spit was

reached. The tide had been ebbing for some hours, and the sand was warm and dry, except near the edge of the water. The canoes were hauled some distance over the sand to a spot where there was a clump of bushes, and where it was reasonable to suppose that they would be perfectly safe even at high tide. A second breakfast was then cooked and eaten, after which the boys set out to explore their camping-ground.

It was simply a low sand-bank, about a hundred feet wide at widest part, and running out two or three hundred feet into the river. As has been said, the north bank of the river was a perpendicular precipice, but now that the tide was out there was a path at the foot of the precipice by means of which any one could walk from the sand-spit to a ravine a quarter of a mile away, and thus reach the meadows lying back of the precipice. This path was covered with water at high tide; but, as it was sure to be passable for three or four hours, Harry and Tom set out to procure provisions for the day.

Log-rolling.

The fleet was wind-bound all that day, for neither the wind nor the sea showed the slightest intention of going down. Harry and Tom returned after an hour's absence, with bread, butter, eggs, milk, and strawberries, and with the cheerful information that, in the opinion of a gloomy farmer, the wind would continue to blow for at least two days more.

After resting and sleeping on the soft sand the boys began to find the time hang heavily on their hands. They overhauled their sails and rigging, putting them in complete order. Charley mended a pair of trousers belonging to Joe in a really artistic way; and Joe, with his left arm in a sling, played "mumble-te-peg" with Harry. Tom collected fire-wood, and, when he had got together more than enough to cook two or three meals, occupied himself by trying to roll a heavy log into a position near the canoes, where it could be used as a seat or a table.

The sand was strewn with logs, big and little, and Harry proposed that as many logs as possible should be got together, so that an enormous camp-fire could be started. It was a happy idea, for it gave the boys employment for the greater part of the day. It became a matter of pride with them to bring the biggest and heaviest of the logs up to the fireplace. Some of them could only be stirred with levers, and moved with the help of rollers cut from smaller logs. Whenever a particularly big log was successfully moved the boys were encouraged to attack a still bigger one. Thus they finally collected an amount of fire-wood sufficient to make a blaze bright enough to be seen a dozen miles at night.

When they were tired of rolling logs Tom went fishing, but caught nothing; while Charley cooked the dinner and watched the rising tide—half afraid that the water would reach the fire and put it out before he could get dinner ready. The tide rose so high that it came within two or three yards of the fire, and almost as near to the canoes, but it spared the dinner. When the tide was nearly full only a small part of the sand-spit was out of water, and the path along the foot of the precipice was completely covered, so that the waves broke directly against the rocks.

"It's lucky for us that the tide doesn't cover the whole of this place," remarked Charley as he placed the dinner on a large log which served as a table, and beat a tattoo on the frying-pan as a signal to Tom to give up fishing and come to dinner. "I should hate to have to take to the canoes again in this wind."

"It's lucky that the tide will ebb again," said Harry, "for we're cut off from the shore as the tide is now, unless we could climb up the rocks, and I don't believe we could."

"It's all right," said Tom, putting his fishing-tackle in his canoe, "provided the tide doesn't come up in the night and float the canoes off."

"Oh, that can't happen!" exclaimed Harry. "The tide's turned already, and doesn't reach the canoes."

"I'm going to sleep on the sand," remarked Joe. "It's softer than the bottom of my canoe, and there isn't any sign of rain."

"You don't catch me sleeping anywhere except in my canoe," said Harry. "There isn't any bed more comfortable than the *Sunshine*."

"Can you turn over in her at night?" asked Joe.

"Well, yes; that is, if I do it very slow and easy."

"The bottom-board is a nice soft piece of wood, isn't it?" continued Joe.

"It's pine-wood," replied Harry, shortly. "Besides, I sleep on cushions."

"And you like to lie stretched out perfectly straight, don't you?"

"I like it well enough—much better than I like to see a young officer trying to chaff his Commodore," returned Harry, trying to look very stern.

"Oh, I'm not trying to chaff anybody!" exclaimed Joe. "I was only wondering if your canoe was as comfortable as a coffin would be, and I believe it is —every bit as comfortable."

When the time came for "turning in" Joe spread his water-proof blanket on the sand close by the side of his canoe. He had dragged her several yards away from the rest of the fleet, so as to be able to make his bed on the highest and driest part of the sand, and to shelter himself from the wind by lying in the lee of his boat. The other boys preferred to sleep in their canoes, which were placed side by side and close together. The blazing logs made the camp almost as light as if the sun were shining, and the boys lay awake a long while talking together, and hoping that the wind would die out before morning.

Joe, whose sprained wrist pained him a little, was the last to fall asleep. While he had expressed no fears about the tide (for he did not wish to be thought nervous), he was a little uneasy about it. He had noticed that when the tide rose during the day it would have completely covered the sand-spit had it risen only a few inches higher. Long after his comrades had fallen asleep it occurred to Joe that it would have been a wise precaution to make the canoes fast to the bushes, so that they could not be carried away; but he did not venture to wake the boys merely in order to give them advice which they probably would not accept. So he kept silent, and toward ten o'clock fell asleep.

In the course of the night he began to dream. He thought that he was a member of an expedition trying to reach the North Pole in canoes, and that he was sleeping on the ice. He felt that his feet and back were slowly freezing, and that a polar-bear was nudging him in the ribs occasionally, to see if he was alive and ready to be eaten. This was such an uncomfortable situation that Joe woke up, and for a few moments could not understand where he was.

The wind had gone down, the stars had come out, and the tide had come up. Joe was lying in a shallow pool of water, and his canoe, which was almost afloat, was gently rubbing against him. He sprung up and called to his companions. There was no answer. The fire was out, but by the starlight Joe could see that the whole sand-spit was covered with water, and that neither the other boys nor their canoes were in sight. The tide was still rising, and Joe's canoe was beginning to float away, when he seized her, threw his blankets into her, and, stepping aboard, sat down, and was gently floated away.

Chapter XII.

JOE was alone on the St. Lawrence in the middle of the night, and with a sprained wrist, which nearly disabled him so far as paddling was concerned. Worse than this, his comrades had disappeared, and there could not be the slightest doubt that their canoes had floated away with them while they were sound asleep. What chance had he of finding them? How could he get ashore, with his sprained wrist; and what probability was there that the three boys thus carried away in their sleep would escape from their dangerous situation without any serious accident?

As these questions presented themselves to Joe his first impulse was to admit that he was completely disheartened and to burst into tears. He was, however, far too manly to yield to it, and he immediately began to think what was the best thing that he could do in the circumstances.

The water was perfectly smooth, so that there was really no danger that the runaway canoes would capsize, unless their owners should start up in a fright and not fully understand that their canoes were no longer on solid land. Neither was there much chance that they would be run down by steamboats, for the steamboat channel was near the south shore of the river, a long distance from the sand-spit. Joe remembered how fast the tide had risen the day before, and he calculated that the missing canoes must have been afloat about half an hour before the water reached the place where he was sleeping. They would naturally drift in the same direction in which the *Dawn* was drifting; and all that it would be necessary for Joe to do in order to overtake them would be to increase the speed at which his canoe was moving.

There was a scarcely perceptible breeze blowing

from the south. Joe got up his main-mast and set his sail. Light as the breeze was, the canoe felt it, and began to move through the water. Joe steered by the stars, and kept the *Dawn* as nearly as possible on the course which he supposed the other canoes had taken. He had no lantern with him, and could see but a little distance ahead in the dark, but he shouted every few moments, partly in order to attract the attention of the missing canoeists, and partly in order to warn any other boat that might be in the neighborhood not to run him down.

After sailing in this way for at least an hour, and hearing no sound whatever but his own voice and the creaking of the canoe's spars, Joe was startled at perceiving a black object just ahead of him. He avoided it with a vigorous movement of his paddle, and as he drifted close to it with the wind shaken out of his sail he saw to his great delight that it was a canoe.

It was the *Sunshine*, with her canoe-tent rigged over her, and her commander sound asleep. Taking hold of her gunwale, Joe drew the two canoes together and put his hand gently on Harry's forehead. Harry instantly awoke, and hearing Joe begging him as he valued his life to lie perfectly still, took the latter's advice, and asked, with some alarm, what was the matter. When he learned that he was adrift on the river he sat up, took down his tent, and getting out his paddle joined in the search for Tom and Charley.

"They must be close by," said Harry, "for all three canoes must have floated away at the same time. Tom and Charley sleep sounder than I do, and if I didn't wake up it's pretty certain that they didn't."

Presently Charley's canoe was overtaken. Charley had been awakened by the sound of Harry's paddle and the loud tone in which Harry and Joe were talking. He was sitting up when the *Dawn* and the *Sunshine* overtook him; and having comprehended the situation in which he found himself on awaking, he was making ready to paddle ashore.

There was now only one canoe missing—the *Twilight*. Harry, Joe, and Charley took turns in shouting at the top of their lungs for Tom, but they could obtain no answer except the echo from the cliffs of the north shore. They paddled up the river until they were certain that they had gone farther than Tom could possibly have drifted, and then turned and paddled down stream, shouting at intervals, and growing more and more alarmed at finding no trace of the lost canoe.

"She can't have sunk, that's one comfort," exclaimed Harry, "for the bladders that Tom put in her at Chambly would keep her afloat, even if he did manage to capsize her in the dark."

"He took the bladders out yesterday morning and left them on the sand just in the lee of his canoe," said Charley. "Don't you remember that he sponged her out after we landed, and that he said that he wouldn't put his things back into her until we were ready to start?"

"I remember it now," replied Harry. "And I

remember that I did the same thing. There's nothing in my canoe now except my water-proof bag and my blankets. But they're not of much consequence compared with Tom. Boys, do you really think he's drowned?"

"Of course he isn't," cried Joe. "We'll find him in a few minutes. He must be somewhere near by, and he's sleeping so sound that he don't hear us. You know how hard it is to wake him up."

"Tom is a first-rate swimmer, and if he has spilt himself out of his canoe and she has sunk, he has swum ashore," said Charley. "My opinion is that we had better stay just where we are until daylight, and then look for him along the shore. He's worth a dozen drowned fellows, wherever he is."

Charley's advice was taken, and the boys waited for daylight as patiently as they could. Daylight—or rather dawn—came in the course of an hour, but not a glimpse of the missing canoe did it afford. The tide had already changed, and the top of the treacherous sand-spit was once more above water, and not very far distant from the canoes. As soon as it was certain that nothing could be seen of Tom on the water his alarmed comrades paddled toward the north shore, hoping that they might find him, and possibly his canoe, somewhere at the foot of the rocks.

They were again unsuccessful. While Joe sailed up and down along the shore, the two other boys paddled close to the rocks, and searched every foot of space where it would have been possible for a canoe to land, or a canoeist to keep a footing above the water. They had searched the shore for a full mile above the sand-spit and had paddled back nearly half the way, when they were suddenly hailed, and looking up, saw Tom standing on a ledge of rock ten feet above the water.

"Are you fellows going to leave me here all day?" demanded Tom. "I began to think you were all drowned, and that I'd have to starve to death up here."

"How in the world did you get up there?"

"HOW IN THE WORLD DID YOU GET UP THERE?"

"Where were you when we came by here half an hour ago?" "Where's your canoe?" "Are you all right?" These and a dozen other questions were hurled at Tom by his excited and overjoyed friends.

"I was asleep until a few minutes ago," replied Tom. "I got up here when the tide was high, and I had hard work to do it, too."

"What's become of your canoe? Is she lost?" asked Harry.

"She's somewhere at the bottom of the river. I tried to turn over in her in the night, thinking she was on the sand-spit, but she turned over with me, and sunk before I could make out what had happened."

"And then you swum ashore?"

"Yes. I saw the north-star, and knew that if I could swim long enough I could find the shore. When I struck these rocks I was disappointed, for I couldn't find a place where I could land until I got my hands on this ledge and drew myself up."

"Unless Tom wants to stay where he is we'd better invent some way of taking him with us," remarked Joe.

"He'll have to get into my canoe," said Harry.

"How deep is the water where you are?" asked Tom.

"It's anywhere from six feet to sixty. I can't touch bottom with the paddle, so it's certain to be more than seven feet deep."

"Then, if you'll please to give me room, I'll jump, and somebody can pick me up."

Tom jumped into the water, and had little trouble in climbing into Harry's canoe—the water being perfectly quiet. The fleet then paddled back to the sand-spit, where they landed and breakfasted, while Tom dried his clothes by the fire.

Every member of the expedition except Joe had lost something, and poor Tom had lost his canoe and everything except the clothes which he was wearing. As long as the water continued to be smooth Tom could be carried in either Harry's or Charley's canoe, but in case the wind and sea should rise it would be very difficult, if not impossible, to keep the canoe right side up with two persons in her. Quebec was still at least twenty-five miles distant, and it would take nearly a whole day of very hard work to paddle a heavy canoe, with two boys in her, only one of whom was furnished with a paddle, twenty-five miles, even in the most favorable circumstances. Moreover, Joe's sprained wrist made it impossible for him to paddle, and the wind was so light that sailing to Quebec was out of the question.

It was therefore decided that Harry should take Joe in the *Sunshine* back to the Jacques Cartier, and leaving him to walk to the nearest railway-station, should return to the sand-spit and join Tom and Charley in paddling down to Quebec, Tom taking Joe's canoe. Although the boys had originally intended to end their cruise at Quebec, they had become so fond of canoeing that they would gladly have gone on to the Saguenay River and, if possible, to Lake St. John; but now that Tom was without a canoe no one thought of prolonging the cruise.

Quebec was reached by the fleet several hours after Joe had arrived there by the train. He was at the landing-place to meet his comrades, and had already made a bargain with a canal-boatman to carry the canoes all the way to New York for five dollars each. As the *Sunshine* was fitted with hatches which fastened with a lock, and as it would be necessary for the Custom-house officer at Rouse's Point to search her, Harry wrote to the Custom-house at that place, giving directions how to open the lock. It was a padlock without a key, one of the so-called letter-locks which can be opened by placing the letters in such a position that they spell some particular word. Harry had provided the canoe with this lock expressly in order to avoid trouble at Custom-houses, and in this instance the plan proved completely successful, for the officer at Rouse's Point was able to unlock the canoe and to lock it up again without a key.

The boys spent a night and a day at Quebec, and, after seeing their canoes safely started, they took the train for New York. As they talked over their cruise on the way home they agreed that canoeing was far more delightful than any other way of cruising, and that they would go on a canoe cruise every summer.

"As soon as I can afford it I shall get a new canoe," said Tom.

"Will you get a 'Rice Laker?'" asked Harry.

"Of course I will. My canoe was much the best boat in the fleet, and I shall get another exactly like her."

"There's no doubt that you are a genuine canoeist, Tom," said Charley. "You've had lots of trouble with your canoe because she had no deck, and at last she sunk and nearly drowned you, because she had no water-tight compartments; but for all that you really think that she was the best canoe ever built. Is everybody else convinced that his own canoe is the best in the world?"

"I am," cried Joe.

"And I am," cried Harry.

"So am I," added Charley; "and as this proves that we are all thorough canoeists, we will join the American Canoe Association at once, and cruise under its flag next summer."

THE END.

www.ingramcontent.com/pod-product-compliance
Lightning Source LLC
Chambersburg PA
CBHW020252170426
43202CB00008B/331